LINCOLN CHRISTIAN COLLEGE

COMMUNITY
101

Also by Gilbert Bilezikian

Christianity 101

Reclaiming the Church

as Community of Oneness

COMMUNITY
101

GILBERT BILEZIKIAN

ZondervanPublishingHouse
Grand Rapids, Michigan

A Division of HarperCollinsPublishers

WILLOW
CREEK
RESOURCES

Community 101
Copyright © 1997 by Gilbert Bilezikian

Requests for information should be addressed to:

⚒ ZondervanPublishingHouse
Grand Rapids, Michigan 49530

Library of Congress Cataloging-in-Publication Data

Bilezikian, Gilbert.
    Community 101: Reclaiming the local church as community of oneness /
Gilbert Bilezikian.
      p.   cm.
    ISBN: 0-310-21741-5 (pbk.)
    1. Church. 2. Community—Religious aspects—Christianity. 3. Christian
leadership. 4. Clergy—Office. I. Title.
BV600.2.B498 1997
262'.7—dc21   97-14458
                                                CIP

All Scripture quotations, unless otherwise indicated, are taken from the *Holy
Bible: New International Version*®. NIV®. Copyright © 1973, 1978, 1984 by
International Bible Society. Used by permission of Zondervan Publishing
House. All rights reserved.

All rights reserved. No part of this publication may be reproduced, stored in a
retrieval system, or transmitted in any form or by any means—electronic,
mechanical, photocopy, recording, or any other—except for brief quotations in
printed reviews, without the prior permission of the publisher.

Printed in the United States of America

00 01 02 03 04 /❖ DH/ 10 9 8 7 6

To God's people at
Willow Creek Community Church,
exemplars of authentic
biblical oneness.

118678

Contents

Foreword

If you had to answer, in a single word, what God's dream for human beings is, what would you say? For anyone who has spent time under the influence of the life and teaching of Gilbert Bilezikian, the answer would be immediate: community. God's dream for the creatures made in his image is that they begin to realize the beautiful words of the psalmist: "How very good and pleasant it is when kindred live together in unity" (Ps. 133:1 NRSV).

Dr. B (as he is known by those of us fortunate enough to be his students and friends) is uniquely qualified to write on this subject. For forty years, the passion of his study as a New Testament professor and scholar has been to understand the nature of biblically functioning community. And this understanding has been tested in the crucible of an actual congregation, for Dr. B has served as a founding elder and a kind of theologian-in-residence for Willow Creek Community Church. So what he says comes from a deep immersion in the text of Scripture and a deep immersion in a flesh-and-blood church.

Here you will find a masterful treatment of God's plan for people to join in radically new community: where servanthood becomes a joyful, mutual way of life, where leadership is worn lightly and offered as a humble gift, where "there is neither Jew nor Greek, slave nor free, male nor female, for you are all one in Christ Jesus" (Gal. 3:28).

As one of his former students, I wish you could hear Dr. B speak on the church in person. To do so is to begin to realize that our human yearning for love and belonging is to be fulfilled through God's "new community," which alone will last forever. The church is not a place for people to gather occasionally for religious services. It is not one more social institution among many others. The church is God's dream for his most cherished creation.

"What is there like the church?" Dr. B asks in his teaching, over and over again. There is nothing—no accomplishment, no organization or country or civilization—there is nothing as important as the church, and only the church will survive history to share in God's eternity. Read these pages and find out for yourself.

John Ortberg

Preface

According to the New Testament, the church of Jesus Christ is the support ("pillar") and the guardian ("bulwark") of God's truth (1 Tim. 3:15 RSV). Unfortunately, history shows that the church has often acted as the enemy and the betrayer of God's revealed truth.

Christians would generally agree that the doctrine of salvation is of paramount importance in their belief system. Yet, as incredible as it may seem, the church lost track of this truth for about a millennium of its existence and replaced it with various theories of salvation by works that never worked. The simple teaching that salvation is a gift of God's grace to be appropriated by faith was finally rediscovered in the sixteenth century.

With a mighty prophetic voice, the whole Bible registers God's opposition to injustice and unrighteousness. However, for the major part of its history, the church has identified itself with institutional evils such as slavery, segregation, racism, sexism, and apartheid, often by misusing texts from Scripture to justify such practices. The church's proven capacity to deviate from the teachings of the Bible is reason for consternation. It also calls for continual reformation.

In our day, there is a clamor for the church to rediscover its identity as community. Many Christian leaders bemoan the fact that the church has lost its basic biblical definition as divinely designed community. Lay people and clergy alike express dissatisfaction with churches conducting their business as if it were a business. They compare the stilted and stultifying routines of their church life to the effervescent explosion of Holy Spirit-generated vitality that enabled the church of Pentecost to conquer the ancient world for Christ. They wonder with nostalgia where the power has gone. They realize that they have often become lost in a jungle-growth of unbiblical traditions that choke the life out of their churches and stifle their ministries. They yearn to rediscover the biblical tradition that preceded their various ecclesiastical traditions. They demand a radical return to the basics of biblical teachings about the church as community.

Three sets of circumstances have converged into the writing of this book. First, its contents reflect biblical insights acquired during thirty years of theological teaching in institutions of higher learning. Second, they also contain the fruit of lessons learned from close personal involvement in the establishment and growth of Willow Creek Community Church and of its affiliated ministries. Finally, they summarize the substance of conferences on the church as community given in the course of a heavy schedule of speaking engagements over the last few years. This book is written partly in response to urgings that the material presented at such conferences be made available in print for the purpose of study and dissemination.

Although this book constitutes a self-contained unit, a thorough study of this teaching on community could begin with my book *Christianity 101* (Zondervan, 1993). In particular, chapter 7, on the doctrine of the church, can be used as a general introduction to the main themes on this topic. The study sequence would then call for reading the present work, *Community 101*, followed by *Beyond Sex Roles* (Baker, 1985), which deals more pointedly with community life in church and family from the perspective of the place of women in those societal contexts. Naturally, the Scriptures remain the supreme guide for a Christian definition of community. Therefore, each of the books mentioned above should be consulted with an open Bible close at hand.

Two dear friends had a part in the making of this book. Kathleen Kegel performed the magic transmutation of a barely legible handwritten text into a high-tech, electronically deliverable, letter-perfect document. Mike Topel screened the manuscript with the same sagacity and unremitting rigor that he had plied into my previous book. I am indebted to a lecture of my former colleague, Dr. David Klopfenstein, for the diagram on page 181.

A few years ago, a group of people advocating a view of women's roles in the church that I consider to be destructive to biblically defined community held a meeting in Chicago and were given air time on a national Christian radio network. During the show, the host phoned me and put me on the line to debate with them some of the issues now covered in this book. As the discussion progressed, it became evident that this group treated with derision the view of community I was defending. It was then that I resolved to put those ideas in writing in order to give them better expression. This book would not have been written without the incentive provided by that incident. Those people will easily recognize themselves and appreciate the significance of this acknowledgment of my indebtedness to their condescension.

At several points in the body of this work, reference is made to the availability of materials on small groups, spiritual gifts, seeker evangelism, and conferences on community. A catalogue of such materials may be obtained at Willow Creek Resources/Zondervan Direct Source, 5300 Patterson Ave. SE, Grand Rapids, MI 49530 (Telephone 1-800-876-7385).

Gilbert Bilezikian

CHAPTER ONE

Only Community Is Forever

Each one of us hides an awful secret. Buried deep within every human soul throbs a muted pain that never goes away. It is a lifelong yearning for that one love that will never be found, the languishing in our inner selves for an all-consuming intensity of intimacy that we know will never be fulfilled, a heart-need to surrender all that we are to a bond that will never fail.

The silent churning at the core of our being is the tormenting need to know and to be known, to understand and to be understood, to possess and to be possessed, to belong unconditionally and forever without fear of loss, betrayal, or rejection. It is the nostalgia for our primal oneness, the silent sorrowing for paradise lost, the age-long pursuit after the encompassing embrace for which we know we were created. It is the search, however wanton and sullied, for the pristine grace of holding and being held, for the freedom to be who we really are without shame or pretense, for release and repose in the womb-like safety of unalterable acceptance and of overarching love.

When we take time to become silent and to listen, we may hear the scream from the depths of our being, the clamor to bare our souls and to reveal the mystery of our true selves. Just listen, listen closely. . . . It is the distant echo of the wail in the garden at the loss of innocence, of the grieving after a remembrance of shared freedom, of the release of body and soul to the embrace of absolute oneness.

Our mourning is for the closeness that was ours by right of creation. Our grief is for the gift lost in the turmoil of rebellion. And now, whenever there is hope, our hope is for paradise regained, for human destiny remade in the redemptive restoration of community, the only certainty of oneness for here and for eternity.

A. THE PRIMACY OF ONENESS

One of the ideas presented in the preceding section is that God offered the gift of oneness to humans when he created them. Indeed, when God formed the original couple, he decreed that "they will become one flesh" (Gen. 2:24).

While this is accurate, it is not the whole truth because oneness existed prior to the creation of humans. Indeed, community finds its essence and definition deep within the being of God. Oneness is primarily a divine mode of being that pertains to God's own existence, independently from and prior to any of his works of creation. Whatever community exists as a result of God's creation, it is only a reflection of an eternal reality that is intrinsic to the being of God. Because God is eternally one, when he created in his image, he created oneness.

1. The Trinity As the Original Community of Oneness

We do not have to go far into the Bible to find a teaching about the nature of God as a community of oneness. Indeed, the first three verses of Genesis reveal that God is a community of three persons in one being.

In Genesis 1:1, we are introduced to God as the grand designer of all creation. He conceives the heavens and the earth in order to bring them into existence. Inasmuch as he generates all that there is, he may be considered the Father of creation. All things find their definition and their origin in him (see also James 1:17).

The second verse describes the activity of another aspect of the being of God, designated as "the Spirit of God." Obviously, this is still a reference to God. But a distinction is made with the specification of "Spirit." Moreover, the activity attributed to the Spirit of God is different from that described in the previous verse in relation to God as "Father." The Spirit does not construct the created world. Instead, he is described as "hovering over" it, once it was set in place. This suggests a function of protector or overseer—in New Testament terms, we might even say he was the "sanctifier" of God's works, bringing to them the blessing of his continued involvement.

In the third verse, we discover a third distinction within the being of God, in the form of the Word of God. It is enough for God to speak the Word, as he says, "Let there be . . . ," and whatever he commands comes into existence through the power of that Word. The Word of God is presented as the executor of God's will, as the agent of creation.

Of course, Christians know that "in the beginning was the Word" and that the Word existed in close association with God. And not only was the Word with God, distinct from him and alongside of him, as it were, but "the Word was God" (John 1:1–2). The Word was completely identified with God in the oneness of their being.

We know from Scripture that all things were made through the Word and that "nothing was made that has been made" without the active involvement of the Word (John 1:3). The story of the beginnings emphasizes eight times the life-giving agency of the Word as God set about to create the universe and all that it contains (Gen. 1:3, 6, 9, 11, 14, 20, 24, 26).

Christians also know that the same Word who was involved in the creation of all things is the one who came in the world as Redeemer, because "the Word became flesh and made his dwelling among us," and he had "the glory of the One and Only, who came from the Father" (John 1:14). The Word is the Son of God.

Thus, one need go only three verses into the Bible to discover what is amply taught in the rest of Scripture, especially in the New Testament, that God is presented as a Tri-unity of divine entities existing as Father, Son, and Holy Spirit, the eternal community of oneness from whom all other communities derive life and meaning. Like Christians, Jews and Muslims also believe in one God. However, because their God is one person within one being, he is the prisoner of his own limitation. Frozen within the singularity of his transcendency, he can never experience community. Not so for the God revealed by Jesus Christ. Although one being, he is eternally three persons within oneness. He values community supremely because he experiences the dynamics and the synergy of three in one. Thus, when he creates in his image, he creates community.

Scripture further teaches that, in this oneness, there is complete mutuality and equality. Otherwise, there would be no oneness. In whatever the Godhead undertakes to do, the three members of the Trinity function together—never independently of each other.

The Father is at the forefront of the work of creation, but both the Word and the Spirit are present and involved with the Father in creation. The Son is at the forefront of the work of redemption, but both the Father and the Spirit are present and involved with the Son in redemption. The Spirit is at the forefront of the work of sanctification, but both the Father and the Son are present and involved in the work of sanctification.

The doctrinal statement of the Evangelical Theological Society describes the biblical teaching about the Godhead as the original community of oneness in a single sentence: "God is a Trinity, Father, Son, and Holy Spirit, each an uncreated person, one in essence, equal in power and glory." Despite its brevity, this marvelous formulation goes to the heart of the matter. It defines the oneness of the Father, Son, and Spirit as pertaining to the essence or being of God. But it also extends this quality of oneness to the activities or functions of the members of the Trinity since they are said to be "equal in power." This summary affirms the essential oneness of the members of the Trinity while disallowing any notion of ranking or of hierarchy among them. Because God is absolute, the oneness of the Trinity is absolute. If any part of the Trinity were less than absolute in essence or in function, the Godhead would also be less than absolute.

For the sake of his redemptive ministry among humans, it became necessary for the Son to relinquish his equality with the Father and to make himself servant to the Father and servant to humans. But this self-humiliation was only temporary. In its eternal state, the divine community is united in absolute oneness, Father, Son, and Holy Spirit, "one in essence, equal in power and glory." (For an expanded discussion of this doctrine, see the Appendix on pages 187–202.)

2. *God's Gift of Oneness to Humans*

God is love. Therefore, he is also a giver, and his giving is done on the scale of infinity. He created the immensity of space and scattered through it hundreds of billions of galaxies, each filled with hundreds of billions of stars—all related to each other by distances conceivable only in terms of innumerable light years.

But God's pet project, as it were, concerned a small planet on the outer fringes of one of those immense galaxies. Having first lavished upon the earth the goodness and the beauty of his creative powers, God proceeded to offer, as a true lover would, his supreme gift: himself.

Obviously, God could not reproduce himself and create another God since he is absolute and, therefore, unique. But God did the next best thing. He created beings in his image. This was the closest he could get to giving of himself without compromising his own divine nature.

So, God actually created a being who was to reflect his own image. But, having done so, he astoundingly declared his creation to be "not good" because it was solitary: God was displeased with the fact that the man was alone (Gen. 2:18). There was one solitary individual, but he had no oneness because there was no one else with whom he could be together in oneness (2:20). Since God is Trinity, he is plurality in oneness. Therefore, the creation in his image required the creation of a plurality of persons. God's supreme achievement was not the creation of a solitary man, but the creation of human community.

In order to do so, God cloned from the solitary human being a rescuer who would bring the emerging image to its rightful dimension of community. A "rescuer for this state of affairs" is the real meaning of "suitable helper" in Genesis 2:20 (cf. v. 18). According to the text, this "helper" (Heb. *'ezer*) was specifically provided so that the man would not remain alone, bereft of community. By himself, he was non-community. God was not satisfied with this situation because the creation of his image required a plurality of persons (cf. 1:26–27). Therefore, the woman was created to "help" the man out of his aloneness so that together they would form the community of oneness.

The notion that "helper" in this passage means an assistant is unwarranted by the context. Some interpreters of the Bible force the modern idea of "helper" as "subordinate worker" into this context. But the Bible never presents the man as if he were overburdened by an excess of work so that he needed an assistant to get things done. It is not as though he was working overtime tending the garden, and God, taking pity on him, provided him with a handmaid whom he could boss around. Such a meaning is totally absent from the account. The *only* reason given in the text for the creation of the woman was to help the man *not to be alone*. The woman was to be the necessary counterpart of the man for the making of community.

In other words, a careful reading of the Genesis text indicates that the "helper" was not provided as a convenience for the man's use, to make his life easier or more pleasant. She was not just a complement to his life, like an adjunct or an afterthought. God made "a helper suitable for him" in relation to the specific situation where it was "not good for the man to be alone" (2:18). The creation of the woman fulfilled God's purpose for the formation of community. While there was only one human being, there was no oneness because there was no community. Oneness finally happened when there were two, who could then become "one flesh" (v. 24). Therefore, to reduce the creation of woman to a complement or addition to the man's otherwise self-sufficient life is to betray a grievous lack of understanding of the biblical doctrine of community.

This higher use of the word "helper" as "rescuer" is amply confirmed throughout the Old Testament. That God is our helper is an important theme of the Bible. But, more pointedly, this word (*'ezer*) is consistently used to describe God's intervention as rescuer in human situations of need (Ex. 18:4; Ps. 33:20; 70:5; 115:9–11; etc.). In this sense, a "helper" is not someone to be used as a convenience but is the condition for survival. Similarly, then, the woman was not given to the man as a convenience, but as the fulfiller of the purpose for which they were both created—the making of the community of oneness.

This richer meaning of "helper" in Genesis 2 is confirmed by the account of the method God used to create the woman. God went out of his way to stage an object lesson that would blazingly demonstrate to the man the woman's essential oneness with him.

Like every other living being on the face of the earth, the man was formed out of the ground (Gen. 1:11–12, 24–25; 2:7). Had the woman been intended to be a mere complement to man, she would also have been formed out of the ground and could have been offered to the man as a servant helper, a sort of live-in housemaid. There would have been no reason for an exceptional creation procedure for the woman. This is exactly what happened when God formed the animals "out of the ground" (2:19) and presented them to the man as "helper" candidates (v. 20). None of them qualified, however.

In order to bring the woman into being, then, God reached deep inside the solitary one, close to his heart, and pulled out of him the other face of the image that had been hidden there. From human life already in existence, God cloned the bones and flesh "helper" who would thereby be empowered to help bring community into reality (vv. 21–23). The man recognized the wonder of this oneness and called the woman by the same name that God had already given her when he "made a *woman*" from the man's side (v. 22). In turn, the man said, "She shall be called *'woman,'* for she was taken out of man" (v. 23).

With this statement, the man emphasized his identity with the woman on two counts. First, they were of the same kind because they shared the same name as the definition of their essential nature—the Hebrew word for "woman" (*ishsha*) is an expanded form of the word for man (*ish*). Second, they shared the same life by virtue of their origin since she was taken out of him.

Scripture thus affirms the full participation of both man and woman in the image of God. The Genesis text never refers to the image of God in relation to the man apart from the woman or vice versa. When God proceeded to create "man" in his image, the recipients of the image were both male and female (1:26–27). The image of God pertained to their humanity rather than to their gender. Since God is spirit, he is not a sexual being. Therefore, he is not bound within his nature by the confinements of gender differentiations. The divine image certainly includes both maleness and femaleness. But it includes much more since it defines everything human that is different from the rest of creation. In particular, the image refers to the fact that God is a divine community of oneness, who creates a human community of oneness as his supreme achievement.

The New Testament teaching about the image of God is consistent with that of the Genesis account. Because originally, man did not come from woman but from God, he reflects the image and glory of God. Because the woman came from the man and was created for man as his helper-rescuer, she obviously shares in that divine image and glory by virtue of her derivation; however, in addition, she also reflects the glory of man from whom she was taken (1 Cor. 11:7–9). The New Testament never contradicts the Genesis text on this score by denying woman's full participation in the image.

There is no indication in the biblical text that the woman was made a lesser person for having been created second or for having been taken out of the man instead of out of the ground. When the man exclaimed, "This is now bone of my bones and flesh of my flesh" (Gen. 2:23), he recognized the woman's full identity with him by saying in effect: "This is another me." He thus emphasized their commonality rather than any alleged complementarity, as if the woman had been created to fill the gaps in his own life. Instead, the biblical text indicates that God created her to fulfill his own purposes for the community of oneness.

The man did not represent 80 percent of the human equation with the woman thrown in as a little complement. Nor did each human represent 50 percent of it, as if God's concern had been for carefully measured equality. Their involvement in the making of community was total, with each pouring into the divinely appointed project 100 percent of what God had invested in him and 100 percent of what God had invested in her for the success of their shared tasks. They were each indispensable to one another as full participants in the establishment of community. In God's economy of oneness, one plus one equals one at the human level (2:24), just as one plus one plus one equals one within the sphere of divine existence.

Consequently, the chronological primacy of the man did not confer on him any advantage of status, rank, or leadership responsibility. In the Genesis creation account, there is no evidence that the man claimed headship or spiritual headship over the woman. The terms "spiritual head" or "spiritual headship" are simply not found in the Bible—much less in the creation account. There are only two lines of authority mentioned in the creation story. One goes from God as sovereign over all creation down to the humans. The other goes from the humans as co-regents over creation, down to their joint dominion over it (1:28). Conspicuously absent from the account is any assignment of a line of authority between the man and the woman.

The New Testament gives the conclusive word on this matter by declaring that "in the Lord" (that is, from a Christian perspective), the fact that woman came from man is evened out by the historical reality that now "man is born of woman." And the Scripture quickly adds, "But everything comes from God" (1 Cor. 11:11–12). Human orderings have only relative significance.

Only God's primacy over everyone and everything else as the source of all life has absolute and lasting value. Complete parity and mutuality are the irreducible conditions for the integrity of biblically defined community.

The Genesis account of creation culminates with two intriguing references that describe the lived-out implications of the oneness of man and woman as a relationship of complete mutuality. The first reference follows immediately the man's recognition of the identity between the woman and himself because she was taken out of him (Gen. 2:23). "For this reason," the text goes on to say—that is, because the woman was separated out of the man—oneness required that they be united again. But this time, in true reciprocity, it is the man's turn to move. He separates out and away from his parents and rejoins the woman. He is "united to his wife" in order to become again one flesh with her (2:24). The process goes full circle as the man's life is now fused to the woman's in order to form again the one flesh entity.

Thus, the mutuality between the man and the woman is complete—to the extent that the man becomes three times servant to the woman. First, he is put to sleep in order to give of himself (literally!) for the woman to receive her being. Second, he leaves his parents for her sake. Third, he brings his life to her. This goes to show again that servanthood and mutual submission constitute the lifestyle, the modus vivendi of oneness relationships.

In the world of the Bible, it was conventionally appropriate for a lesser person to go to the one who held a higher position. In this case, it is the man who moves away and gravitates toward his wife, to whom he "cleaves" or "clings" (RSV, NRSV). Before sin came into the world, there was no concern with structures of authority among humans and no need for such—only complete reciprocity. Therefore, the movement of the man toward the woman does not carry connotations of his subordination. Neither the man nor the woman is the ruling head of their union. They are united in a relationship of undefiled oneness.

The second reference concerns the dress code in the garden, or the lack thereof (2:25). "Both" the man and the woman were naked and "felt no shame." Rather than reflecting negatively on the human body, the author of Genesis makes this reference to shame because, in biblical tradition, to go naked was a shameful condition. It was a sign of weakness, subordination, or destitution. Slaves, captives, and beggars were naked. As such, they were objects of derision. But because there was no disparity between the man and the woman, both were naked in the garden of innocence. One was not higher or better than the other. They were both servants together under the authority of God and, therefore, servant to each other. As a result, neither was ashamed to be naked.

Only after the sin of rebellion committed by the man and the woman had entered their world were their eyes opened to their former status of mutual servanthood. Having now ceased to be servants, they improvised wretched coverings to hide the pride that had replaced their oneness (Gen. 3:7). Even more tragically, their oneness was also replaced by a relationship of authority and subjection as man became the ruler (3:16).

Thankfully, according to the New Testament, the servant relationship that was lost in the garden is recovered in the new community. It becomes the hallmark of the way Christians relate to each other. In both church and family, the two communities of oneness generated by the redemptive ministry of Christ, the mode of interaction between its members is reciprocal servanthood and, therefore, mutual submission (Matt. 20:25–28; Gal. 5:13; Phil. 2:3–8). Accordingly, men and women in Christian community do not complement each other within an order of authority, but they minister together and to each other in an order of mutual submission and of servant reciprocity (Eph. 5:21). Thus was recovered the gift of community that had been offered by the Creator to humans at the dawn of history.

3. The Expansion of Community

The making of community was reason enough for creation. But if community is God's highest aim, it deserves to be expanded. So, God gave two directives to the humans for the proper increase of community. Their first assignment was to have children and to raise them so that they would also become reproductive and fill the earth. Their second task was to take care of the earth, to rule it and subdue it (Gen. 1:28). Those two mandates are closely related since the task of populating the earth requires its careful management. The first task relative to children may be called the domestic mandate; the second, the dominion mandate.

Because both of those tasks pertain to the development of community, they were deemed important enough to require the full participation of both humans in carrying them out. It was not as if one was put in charge of the domestic duty and the other of the dominion function according to some predetermined role assignments. God directed both the man and the woman to be fruitful and to increase in number, and both to subdue the earth and to rule over creation. That is, both mandates required male and female human beings to be full participants in the building of community and to share leadership in its management.

It is sometimes assumed that predetermined role distinctions can be derived from the male/female differentiation that exists between humans. Obviously, the biological functions of pregnancy, birthing, and suckling meant that the woman had a unique contribution to make in the accomplishment of the domestic mandate. Likewise, the man had a greater contribution to make in regard to the dominion mandate since he would not experience the constraints of childbearing and breast-feeding.

However, the fact that men and women bring different gifts to their common stewardship does not imply the superiority of one over the other, the leadership of one and the subjection of the other, or the right of one to exercise authority over the other. No man or woman may assume to have the gift of leadership in all areas of life simply by virtue of being male or female. Among mutually submitted and servant-minded individuals, gift-specific leadership is offered and accepted on the basis of competency rather than other considerations such as rank or gender.

As we shall discover in our discussion of community in the New Testament, total participation of all through the stewardship of each one's spiritual gifting is an essential trait of the community of oneness. The imposition of restrictions and exclusions to ministry on the basis of role structures inhibits the expansion of authentic community. From the very beginning, God ordained that the making and the growth of community be the shared responsibility of all members of community.

As noted above, community as God ordained it was not an incidental concern of his nor did it happen haphazardly as the serendipitously creative result of a transcendental cosmic brainstorm. Community is deeply grounded in the nature of God. It flows from who God is. Because he is community, he creates community. It is his gift of himself to humans.

Therefore, the making of community may not be regarded as an optional decision for Christians. It is a compelling and irrevocable necessity, a binding divine mandate for all believers at all times. It is possible for humans to reject or alter God's commission for them to build community and to be in community. But this may happen only at the cost of forsaking the Creator of community and of betraying his image in us; this cost is enormous, since his image in us is the essential attribute that defines our own humanity.

B. THE CENTRALITY OF ONENESS

It is one of the laws of spiritual life, as inexorable as a mathematical axiom, that the survival and welfare of authentic community are dependent on the members of community being in communion with God, since he is the creator of community. In order to be attuned to each other in oneness, humans must be individually attuned to God because he is himself oneness and the designer of human oneness. Therefore, the quality and the viability of human communities vary in response to the members' willingness to accept their own dependency on God.

1. *The Loss of Oneness*

The fact that human community is grounded deep within the being of God is well illustrated by the events in the Garden of Eden. As long as the man and the woman were in right relationship with God, they were in oneness together. The moment they violated their relationship with God by turning their backs on him and going their own way, their oneness was shattered. Not only did sin separate humans from God, it also separated them from each other. In their state of innocence, the first humans found no offense in walking around the garden naked and without shame (Gen. 2:25). The baring of their beings to each other and the sharing of their sexual mutuality was perfectly acceptable to them as an essential expression of their oneness in reciprocal servanthood.

However, when they broke their communion with God, they discovered that their own relationship had broken down. The display of their physical differences had been a welcome and visible sign of their mutual submission. Now, it became intolerable, and their eyes were opened to that which made them different. What had been a means of bonding became a rupture. This alienation forced them to cover themselves with makeshift garments, and each became an island unto oneself (3:7). The male/female differentiation that had made possible the physical expression of their oneness became the focal point of their broken relationship. Divorced from its creational source, what God had given as a blessing became a curse.

The most grievous casualty of the humans' rebellion against God and their severance from him as their source was that each of them became dependent on the element from which he or she had been taken. The man had been made from "the dust of the ground" (2:7); he became a slave to the ground. That is, his destiny was to remain in subjection to the ground as to a cruel taskmaster until the ground would eventually claim his life (3:17–19). The woman had been made from the man (2:22); she became slave to him as indicated by God's statement: "Your desire will be for your husband" (3:16). That is, she would aspire to have him again as the servant partner she knew in the goodness of their oneness; instead, he would "rule over" her. She would reach out to him in the context of the pain she would experience as a woman. Instead of tenderness, she would meet with dominance.

The other casualty of their rebellion was the loss of their oneness. The full parity and the harmonious relationship of mutuality they enjoyed before the Fall was replaced by their hideous opposite: the ruler/subject hierarchy. God's original design of oneness for his creatures became shattered by the sin-rebellion, appropriately called "the Fall" in religious tradition. Oneness was supplanted by the principle of rulership of man over woman, a grievous violation of God's will for them since it resulted from the Fall, itself the supreme violation of God's will.

A measure of the relational disaster that resulted from the Fall is given by the separation of the man and the woman in regard to the tasks that God had earlier assigned for them to carry out together. In the days of the Garden, the oneness of the couple was expressed in their shared responsibility to fulfill the domestic and dominion mandates together. The breakdown of oneness put an end to their cooperative involvement in those tasks.

Their separation was so radical that the man and woman also became separated according to role distinctions. After the Fall, the dominion mandate devolved to the man as he faced a lifetime of subsistence at the cost of struggle and pain (3:17–19). The only reference to the domestic mandate after the Fall also describes childbearing as a painful process that the woman would have to experience alone (v. 16).

The man and the woman found themselves separated from each other, isolated in their pain, locked into separate roles, and caught in a structure of hierarchy that demeaned both. The fact that, in some cultures, women carry alone the responsibilities for both childbearing and subsistence goes to show how susceptible is the practice of rulership to abuse.

The breakdown of community and its degradation into hierarchy had devastating effects on human relationships. The beautiful community of oneness designed by God was replaced by monstrous, dehumanizing institutions that resulted from Satan's nefarious work in the Garden. Some of them even forced their way into the structures of the old covenant.

The one-on-one marriage relationship established by God at the beginning gave way to the practice of polygamy, whereby one man could own several wives. Spiritual hall-of-famers such as Abraham, Jacob, Gideon, and David collected wives like chattel (Gen. 25:1–6; 29:21–30; 30:4, 9; Judg. 8:30–31; 2 Sam. 3:2–5; 5:13–16). Even the common man could own more than one wife (cf. Ex. 21:10; Deut. 21:15).

By definition, the one-flesh relationship created by God could not be severed. Once it became replaced by hierarchy, however, women became disposable objects as well as collectible commodities. As a result, no-fault divorce for males only became institutionalized so that a husband could repudiate his wife for any reason or without a reason. The wife had no recourse for appeal. On the other hand, a wife could not divorce her husband under any circumstances, regardless of the amount of abuse and treachery meted out to her. She was totally at the mercy of her ruler-husband (Deut. 24:1–4).

The pattern of male rulership that issued from the Fall became legislated as a patriarchal system within which the primal male of a household was its absolute master. Within this hierarchy, a woman, whether single or married, was treated like a child. Her decisions and commitments could be overruled at will by her father or husband (Num. 30:5, 8, 13). As such, a mother suffered the humiliation of finding herself at the same level of subjection to the authority of her husband as her own daughter (v. 16). The Fall caused divinely instituted oneness to be sacrificed on the altar of hierarchy.

Such was the devastation that resulted from the sin in the Garden of Eden that the one-flesh principle, God's supreme creational achievement, is never mentioned again in the Old Testament after Genesis 2. Oneness had been replaced by the "hardness of heart." It would be restored for the proper structuring of the communities of redemption only with the coming of the Savior (Matt. 19:4–8). He would make all things new again and restore the community of oneness in fulfillment of God's original purposes in Eden.

In the meantime, God and humans would have to live with the consequences of the Fall. What little was left of community kept disintegrating on an even broader scale. This general decadence led humans to the fateful decision to build the Tower of Babel (Gen. 11:1–8). At first sight, it might appear that their project to build a city was in conformity to the ideal of community—a lot of people brought together to live in one place. But the text reveals that the motivations were wrong. The men said, "Let us build ourselves a city" (v. 4). They were not building a community under God, according to his designs; their enterprise was totally humanistic. They were putting themselves at its center— not God and his will. Their purpose was to reach into the heavens and to make a name for themselves. This idolatrous endeavor not only excluded God, but it was designed to defy him with the puny power of human technology.

However, the effort became counterproductive. The tower builders became scattered over all the earth, and when they tried to communicate among themselves, they could not understand each other's speech (vv. 8–9). There can be no community without communication. In their attempt to build a false community based on faked oneness, they lost the very capacity to speak to each other about community.

2. The Recovery of Oneness

If God were a quitter, the story might have ended at this point. But the Bible insists that God is love. As a true lover, God never gives up on those he loves. He never jettisoned his eternal project of community building. Out of the wreckage of the old community, he drew a new community.

In order to realize this plan, God chose a man called Abram (Gen. 12:1–3). He commanded him to leave his ancestral home so that he could break away from the old, corrupted community in which he lived and lay the foundations for the making of the new community. To that effect, God gave Abram the promise of a personal blessing ("I will bless you"), which would translate into a national blessing ("I will make you into a great nation"). The purpose of the personal and national blessings would, in turn, bring about a universal blessing to benefit all humanity ("all peoples on earth will be blessed through you"). By leaving his old, broken-down community and by going toward a land of promise, Abram accepted God's plan for him to spearhead the establishment of the new community that would eventually bring together, in the church, believers from all the peoples of the earth.

First, God tested Abram to determine whether he would be open to enter into communion with him and, thus, be the one to reestablish the relationship that humans were created to have with God. Abram was approved, and he became the model of faith for all believers of all times (Gen. 15:6; Rom. 4:6).

Then, because of Abram's obedience, God gave him a new identity suitable for his role as the originator of the new community (Gen. 17:1–8). God changed his name from Abram, which means "exalted father" of one people, to Abraham, which means "father of many" nations. God explained the reason for this change as he told Abraham, "I have made you the ancestor of a multitude of nations" (v. 5 NRSV).

Along with a new identity, Abraham received an everlasting covenant of blessing from God (a binding spiritual contract), which would cover all his descendants for generations to come (Gen. 17:7). With this solemn transaction, God used Abraham not only to reintroduce into the fallen world the principle of personal communion with God through faith in him, but he also used Abraham and his believing descendants from a multitude of nations as a bridgehead on the human scene to create the universal new community, called "the church" in the New Testament.

The story of how this promised covenant fared among the direct ethnic descendants of Abraham is a tale of unrelenting disasters, described at length in the Old Testament. God faithfully kept his end of the covenant, but human beings had become corrupted beyond the hope of reclamation by the anti-community forces that had been unleashed at the Fall. Even with the benefits of father Abraham as the model of faith, of God's covenant with them, of the gift of godly leaders, judges, and prophets to guide them in the ways of God, the nation fell into repeated cycles of rebellion, apostasy, defeats, invasions, divisions, and exiles until, mercifully, "when the time had come, God sent his Son, born of a woman" (Gal. 4:4 NRSV).

Often during this somber period, God's ideal of community seemed to have been lost. Many times, it only hung by a thin thread of hope. But ultimately, God's dream prevailed, and the Redeemer came. Through his ministry on earth, he established an unshakable foundation for the building of God's new community.

At the center of history, over the rubble of failed human community, stands the towering form of the cross. The very shape of the cross suggests the two main transactions that were effected through it. The upright post stands for the restoration of our communion with God. On that tree Christ died, giving his life for the forgiveness of our sins. In that death, God was reaching down from the holiness of his transcendence above, down into the abyss of our human need in order to reconcile us to himself. This vertical dimension symbolizes the need and the potential of every human being to enter into a saving relationship with God through Christ. Our individual response of acceptance to God's offer of reconciliation through the cross of Christ reestablishes that communion with him for which we had been created, but which was forfeited in the Garden and which we keep on rejecting individually with our own cumulative sinfulness. The vertical segment of the cross is the channel that conveys God's forgiving grace to receptive sinners and transforms them into live elements of the new community.

Many Christians think that having a personal relationship with God through Christ is all there is to Christianity. They are sorely mistaken, for there is that other dimension to the cross. The vertical trunk by itself does not make a cross. There is also the horizontal beam, appropriately called the crossbar.

The arms of Jesus were stretched on that horizontal rack, and his servant hands were nailed to it. But because Christ died for all of us, and because we all matter equally to him, his extended arms reach out from the crossbeam to all who want reconciliation with God in order that we may be reconciled also to one another and be brought together to form one body in his embrace of love. As a result, Christ can form the new community—a new oneness—by making peace and by reconciling us all to God in one body through the cross, through which he put to death our mutual hostility (Eph. 2:13–18).

All the designs of God for the creation of the new community are achieved through the cross. Those who were far away are "brought near through the blood of Christ" (Eph. 2:13). He has made us one by "abolishing in his flesh" (v. 15) the obstacles to community. And "through the cross" (v. 16), he reconciled us into one body by bringing to an end our alienation and hostility. The cross, in other words, not only provides for our reconciliation to God in its vertical dimension, but it also makes possible reconciliation among humans with its horizontal embrace.

Aware of the dual dimension of his teaching about reconciliation with God and among humans, a sly opponent of Jesus once tried to embarrass him publicly by forcing him to choose one dimension, "Teacher, which is the greatest commandment in the Law?" (Matt. 22:36). Jesus answered that there were two great commandments—not just one: love God with all you have and love your neighbor as yourself—which also means, love your neighbor with all you have (vv. 37–39).

The first great commandment relates to the vertical dimension of the cross; it has to do with our relationship to God. The other great commandment pertains to the horizontal dimension of the cross; it concerns life in community. One piece of timber without the other does not make a cross. Conversely, neither of the two great commandments without the other fulfills the will of God. Genuine communion with God translates in active participation into the building of community. It is impossible to love God without loving our neighbor since, in the actual practice of love, our service to God can only find expression in our service to others. To emphasize the importance of these two great commandments, Jesus claimed that they summarize his own teaching and encompass God's entire revelation (v. 40). What God wants us to know of the whole Bible is rightly represented in the two great commandments.

This correlation of the two great commandments with the two dimensions of reconciliation symbolized by the structure of the cross demonstrates the centrality of community in God's design. The making of community cannot be a side issue or an optional matter for Christians. It is as important to God as one's individual salvation. Without community, there is no Christianity. Perfect community is to be found at the intersection of the two segments of the cross, where those who are reconciled with God can be reconciled together. Community is central to God's purposes for humankind.

3. The Prayer for Oneness

When the earthly ministry of Jesus drew near to its tragic end, he gathered his followers for one last meal together. The disciples feared an impending disaster. Jesus knew already what it was: a cross on Mount Calvary. The moment was charged with emotion and heavy with sadness. Jesus opened his heart to them and spoke to them freely (John 13–16). Then, he prayed (ch. 17). A few hours later, he would pray again, privately to his Father, in the relative seclusion of the Garden of Gethsemane. That was generally how he liked to pray—but not so for this prayer in the Upper Room. Although he was in close communion with the Father, he wanted to share his prayer with the disciples. So, he prayed audibly in their presence. They listened intently and registered his prayer in their memory.

Because this was Christ's last meeting with his followers, the Upper Room prayer represents a summation of his whole ministry, a legacy that he entrusted to the Father in the presence of his followers as witnesses. As history was rushing toward its focal point in his redemptive death, the persistent concern Christ expressed in his prayer was for the oneness of his followers (John 17:11, 20–23).

Jesus appropriately petitioned the Father for the protection of his followers. However, the request for protection was not to spare them from danger, want, or even persecution. The purpose of God's protection was to enable them to achieve among themselves the same kind of oneness that prevailed between Father and Son within the Trinity. Indeed, Jesus prayed, "Holy Father, protect them . . . so that they may be one as we are one" (v. 11).

The oneness that Jesus was praying for was not mere unity. It was the oneness that reaches deep into the being of God and finds its source in the relation between Father and Son. Jesus was asking for the restoration among humans of the oneness that had originally been entrusted to them in creation, a oneness made in the image of the oneness within the Trinity (Gen. 2:24). For Jesus, the model for oneness among humans was nothing less than that found in the relationship between Father and Son (John 17:11, 21, 22). Referring to their oneness, the Son could boldly exclaim to the Father, "You are in me and I am in you," and he could pray for all of his followers to be one to the same extent and with the same intensity (v. 21).

Christ's concern for oneness in this last prayer was not limited to his immediate disciples. It extended to all believers of all times throughout the future of the church. Referring to his disciples, he said, "My prayer is not for them alone. I pray also for those who will believe in me through their message" (v. 20). This includes all those through the ages who have been reached redemptively by the gospel—"that all of them may be one, Father, just as you are in me and I am in you" (v. 21). Christ desired that his church would be the earthly community of oneness modeled after the eternal community of oneness.

Jesus went on to declare that he had provided his followers with everything they needed to bring about this oneness. He prayed, "I have given them the glory that you gave me, that they may be one as we are one" (v. 22). All the resources the Father had entrusted to the Son were now made available to his followers for the purpose of creating the new community of oneness.

Despite this almost embarrassingly repetitious insistence on oneness, Jesus went on praying, "that they may become completely one, so that the world may know that you have sent me" (v. 23 NRSV). Just prior to his sacrifice on the cross, Jesus' heart ached for his followers to band together in communities that would reflect authentic oneness so that their witness to the world would be effective.

This concern for the survival of the church down through the ages provides the explanation for the anguished tones of Jesus' prayer. He knew that if the church should fail to demonstrate community to the world, it would fail to accomplish its mission because the world would have reason to disbelieve the gospel (vv. 21, 23). According to that prayer, the most convincing proof of the truth of the gospel is the perceptible oneness of his followers.

In our day, whenever the church is ineffective and its witness remains unproductive, the first questions that must be raised are whether the church functions as authentic community and whether it lives out the reality of its oneness. In a community-starved world, the most potent means of witness to the truth of the gospel is the magnetic power of the oneness that was committed by Christ to his new community at the center of history.

C. THE FINALITY OF ONENESS

Jesus spent the last hours before his betrayal with his disciples. He ended their time together with a prayer, the main burden of which was his yearning for the oneness of his followers down through the ages (John 17:11, 20–23; note v. 20). Then, his vision arched over his time of suffering and death to anticipate the divine glory that he would recover in his oneness with the Father, the same glory he had before he came into the world—in fact, even before the creation of the world (v. 24). This final petition was framed within this perspective of eternal life. He yearned for the church to join him in eternity and to share in the contemplation of the glorious oneness in heaven. This was the ultimate blessing, the final destination of his followers. Jesus prayed for "[them] to be with me where I am."

1. The End

Jesus often taught about events surrounding the ending of history. He predicted that the time would come when "the dead will hear the voice of the Son of God and those who hear will live" (John 5:25). Whenever Jesus spoke of the resurrection of believers, he described it as one final collective event, as a universal gathering that would transit all of them into eternity together as a community re-formed (Matt. 13:47–49; 24:30–31; John 5:28–29).

Unfortunately, many Christians think of their salvation after death as a solo flight to heaven, where they will make individual entrances at the pearly gates. The Bible teaches precisely the opposite—that is, the passage of believers into eternity will take the form of one mass migration from this world into the next. When the Lord comes down from heaven to terminate history with his universal command and with the victorious trumpet call of God, believers who had died along the centuries will instantly come back to life and, together with the believers alive at the time, will be gathered up together to be with the Lord forever (1 Thess. 4:15–17). This sounds more like one giant jumbo-jet trip than scattered solo flights! In this manner, God's people on earth will be transferred into eternity as one body, a fully formed community.

For a representation of the church in the world, the New Testament uses the symbolism of a radiant bride, anticipating its union with Christ in heaven (2 Cor. 11:2). Because Christ loves and serves the church as a husband loves and serves his bride, he is busy making "her holy ... to present her to himself as a radiant church, without stain or wrinkle or any other blemish" (Eph. 5:26–27). The apostle Paul described as a "profound mystery" the correlation that exists between the relationship of Christ with the church on the one hand, and, on the other, the oneness of man and woman as God binds them in the one flesh relationship from the beginning (v. 32). The basic community on earth, in other words—that of man and woman bonded in oneness—reflects the reality of the ultimate community in heaven, the glorified church united with the Savior.

2. *The New Jerusalem*

The heavenly union thus being prepared throughout history is described as a festive event in the visions of the End. While evil forces are being destroyed on earth, the sound of the roar of "a great multitude" in heaven announces the celebration of the "wedding supper of the Lamb" (Rev. 19:6–9). In case one should not know who the bride is, the text offers a subtle identification to the effect that the bride collectively is "the saints"—the redeemed people of the earth who are given to wear the "fine linen, bright and clean," which stands for their "righteous acts."

The "bride beautifully dressed for her husband" is evoked again in the story of the passing away of our universe (Rev. 21:1–3). The old heaven and earth are replaced with a new reality because history has spent its course and the scroll of time has been rolled out with none left to go. The last act of the human drama has been played out and the lights go off.

The galaxies, suns and moons, the solar system, and the earth all disappear into a terminal black hole. Even the sea, which had been a primordial element of creation, is gone. At creation, "long ago by God's word the heavens existed and the earth was formed out of water and by water" (2 Peter 3:5). Now, at the End, by the same word of God, everything is vaporized out of existence, including the generative sea. The heavens disappear with a roar; the elements are destroyed by fire, and the earth and everything in it are cremated (v. 10). The sin-polluted systems of this world are purged away without regret because it is replaced by a reality so beautiful that it makes the old universe pale into insignificance.

This new reality comes out of heaven, from the very hands of God. It is his supreme creation, and it looks as beautiful as a holy bride prepared for her husband. It is the Holy City, the new Jerusalem (Rev. 21:2). A city is a picture of community, with a lot of people living close together in one place. It is the community of oneness created by God.

Although it is called the "new Jerusalem," this city has nothing to do with the old Jerusalem in Palestine, a place of bondage and hatred that has disappeared in the terminal conflagration of the universe. This is the Jerusalem from above, the spiritual mother of all God's children, the community of the redeemed according to God's promise to Abraham (Gal. 4:26–28). It is the Holy City because God made it (Heb. 11:10). It is the city of the living God, the church of the firstborn whose names are written in heaven, where live the spirits of the righteous made perfect and where thousands upon thousands of angels exult in joyful assembly. Of course, God, the judge of all, is there, but also Jesus, the mediator of the salvation acquired with his blood (12:22–24). This is the city of our God, the new Jerusalem, which is coming down out of heaven from God (Rev. 3:12).

This spiritual Jerusalem is the church, God's new creation— not a place built by human hands, but a community made by him and brought to eternal safety under his watchcare. The old, earthly Jerusalem, with the temple at its center, was the gathering place for worship for the old covenant people. The heavenly community is also called Jerusalem because it is the final and permanent gathering of the new people of God (Rev. 21:3). There is no temple there as there was at the center of the old, defunct Jerusalem because the Lord God Almighty and the Lamb are its temple (v. 22).

Should any doubt remain concerning the identity of the heavenly Jerusalem as God's church transferred from earth to glory, the Scriptures invite us to contemplate the Holy City one last time (Rev. 21:9–22:5). The sight is breathtaking. Once more, the Holy City, Jerusalem, is described coming down out of heaven. Since it is entirely the work of God, it shines with the glory of God. The continent-size dimensions of the city defy the capacities of human imagination to visualize it. The city is a cube of solid gold 1,400 miles high and wide. If it were a physical structure sitting on land, it would obliterate the Middle East off the map, and its top would reach a height over two hundred times the altitude at which jetliners usually cruise in the stratosphere. There would be enough space on its top side to fit two million cities the size of Jerusalem in New Testament times. At that height, the temperature would be 500 degrees below zero and, of course, there would be no air to breathe.

Obviously, the fantastical description of the city is intended to represent a spiritual reality of infinitely greater significance than a physical structure, as grandiose as it could be. Actually, the description of the city contains several clues to indicate that the symbolism represents a spiritual reality. The city bears the names of the twelve tribes of Israel and of the twelve apostles of the Lamb as representations of the totality of the people of God from both old and new covenant (21:12, 14). The temple of the city is not a building, but the Lord God and the Lamb are its temple, both spiritual beings (v. 22). The Lamb is the lamp of the city (v. 23). Just as the church is represented under the symbolism of a city, so the spiritual presence of Christ is symbolized by an animal (Lamb) and an object (lamp), neither of which should be interpreted physically. The nations and the kings, probably those who were promised as descendants to Abraham, are in the city (21:24; 22:2; cf. Gen. 17:6). The servants of God and of the Lamb will serve him, and they will reign forever and ever (Rev. 22:3, 5). The city is exclusively for those whose names are written in the Lamb's book of life (21:27) and who have washed their robes (22:14).

As valuable as these indications are, the indisputable identification of the heavenly city as the church is given at the beginning of the story. An angel said, "Come, I will show you the bride, the wife of the Lamb" (21:9). And he showed "the Holy City, Jerusalem, coming down out of heaven from God. It shone with the glory of God" (vv. 10–11). This simple equation of the Holy City with the "bride, the wife of the Lamb" is the decisive clincher to a biblical theme that started with Abraham.

When Abraham arrived in the land that had been promised to him, he never claimed it as his own or for his descendants. He lived on it like a nomadic stranger. This was because, beyond the land, he was looking "forward to the city with foundations, whose architect and builder is God" (Heb. 11:8–10). This city was not to be built on earth with human hands, but by God himself in the spiritual realm. So neither Abraham nor his descendants received the promise that was to be fulfilled in Christ and in his church. They only saw it on the horizon of faith and recognized it from a distance (v. 13). Through the eyes of faith, they perceived that God had "prepared a city for them" (v. 16), a community made of all Abraham's believing "descendants as numerous as the stars in the sky and as countless as the sand on the seashore" (v. 12).

With the church universal, these spiritual descendants all "have come to Mount Zion, to the heavenly Jerusalem, the city of the living God . . . the church of the firstborn, whose names are written in heaven" (Heb. 12:22–23). Because they "worship God acceptably with reverence and awe," they receive "a kingdom that cannot be shaken" or conquered (v. 28). In this world, there is no city that has eternally enduring significance, "but we are looking for the city that is to come" (13:14).

Thus, the Scriptures bring the theme of the city to spectacular closure with the vivid image of the church as the heavenly city built and indwelt by God. The vision described on the last page of the book of Revelation suggests three crucial lessons in regard to the church as community (Rev. 21:1–22:5).

First, the lavish description of the city's decorations, of its walls and foundations covered with all kinds of gems, and of the city itself made of a single block of pure gold fourteen hundred miles high and wide, figuratively suggests an enormous divine investment of resources in the making of the church. For God, the church is the centerpiece of history. He draws all that is dear and durable from the world and from the passing generations to gather a pilgrim people destined to be the showcase of his grace for eternity.

To this magnificent project, he devotes all that he has, including the gift of himself in the person of his Son. Obviously, this one historical investment alone is more valuable than a million

Himalayas of solid gold covered with diamonds. Gold can do nothing for our soul's salvation. Only the sacrificial death of the Savior could obtain it. Because of it, "God raised us up with Christ and seated us with him in the heavenly realms in Christ Jesus, in order that in the coming ages he might show the incomparable riches of his grace, expressed in his kindness to us in Christ Jesus" (Eph. 2:6–7). In other words, from a divine perspective, the formation of that community of oneness is what history is all about. Like a bride to her husband, the church is God's most precious possession. The making of the church justified his most costly investment and his dearest sacrifice.

The second lesson to be drawn from the vision reinforces the first. Because of the pollution of sin, this universe is doomed to extinction. The heavens and the earth will pass away and the sea will be no more. This old order will be replaced by a new reality but for one exception—the church, God's age-long dream for a community of oneness. "In the end the whole of created life will be rescued from the tyranny of change and decay, and have its share in that magnificent liberty which can only belong to the children of God" (Rom. 8:21 PHILLIPS). Everything within history that has eternal value will be transferred into eternity in the form of community.

The third lesson has to do with the most important thing that God is doing in this world. Obviously, divine providence is operative in many areas of life. In fact, the whole world is sustained by God's word of power (Heb. 1:3). But, as we have briefly traced it in Scripture, God has one priority project throughout history, one that he will bring to climactic completion at the end of history—the formation of the new community. Since community alone will survive from this world into the next, it is ultimately the only thing God is doing today that has eternal significance.

The foregoing survey has made it clear that, according to Scripture, community is not a human invention or a mere social convention, or even less a solution of desperation for group survival. Community is God's dearest creation because it is grounded in his nature and reflects his true identity as a plurality of persons in oneness of being. Moreover, the establishment of community was God's dream for his creation from the very beginning, and he has pursued it all along history and will continue to do so to the very end of time. This dream will be fulfilled when the church is ushered from time into eternity, to be united as a bride to her husband in the Savior's embrace of redemptive love.

Consequently, matters pertaining to the maintenance, growth, and expansion of the church must be of supreme importance to its members. Whether community happens or not may not be left to chance. Christians are under obligation to make it happen, and to make it happen as God intends community to be, not according to their own traditions and preferences, and certainly not according to alien patterns of non-community imported into the church from a world that is itself bereft of the joy of authentic community and yearning for it.

Therefore, it behooves Christians to draw, not from their own experiences and traditions but from Scripture, accurate definitions of community and of its workings, to examine each of their communal practices under the microscope of God's Word in order to test its biblical nature, to eliminate ruthlessly traditional accretions that hinder true community, and to replace them with elements of authentic community, biblically defined.

The remainder of this book is devoted to the definition of such components of community, mainly on the basis of New Testament teachings. They may serve as a grid to evaluate the biblical nature of existing practices, to provide guidance in bringing faulty practices in line with biblical teaching, and to assist in laying a biblical foundation for the planting of new fellowships and churches as communities of oneness.

CHAPTER TWO

Oneness

A visual representation of oneness may be created instantly by clasping one's hands together. The hands are separate entities, each distinctively independent from the other. Yet the interlocked fingers of one's clasped hands suggests a bonding that makes of them one body. After creating man and woman from one body, God declared them united into one flesh (Gen. 2:22–24). This joining together of two independent lives into oneness provides the basic model for biblical community. While praying to the Father, the Son described their own oneness as "you in me and I in you." He asked for exactly the same oneness to prevail among his followers (John 17:21).

A. ATTACK ON COMMUNITY

The brutal separation caused by sin may be illustrated by wrenching apart the clasped hands. This subversion of oneness was the result of the Fall, the work of Satan (Gen. 3:7). Unfortunately, the damage inflicted on oneness was far greater than mere separation. It led to ruler/subject hierarchy (v. 16). This tragedy may be enacted with one hand made into a fist over the other.

The exercise is simple, like a Sunday School action song—

Hands clasped: God loves oneness
Hands apart: Satan hates oneness
Fist over palm: Satan loves rulership

Fortunately, rulership is not the end of the story because, wherever the gospel reaches, there exists the potential for oneness to happen again. The gospel is the message of salvation—that, through the cross, we have peace with God and are reconciled to him (Col. 1:20). But the gospel is also the good news of the restoration of community because, through the same cross, we all become one body (Eph. 2:16). God's dream for a community of oneness can still prevail over separation and rulership. Satan will not always have the upper hand; hands may be clasped again.

Whenever oneness occurs, however, it swiftly comes under attack from savage anti-community forces loose in the world. Much of the history reported in the Bible demonstrates how difficult it is for humans, even under the protection of divine guidance, to establish and to maintain community. The repeated failures of the old covenant people and the difficulties faced by early congregations, such as those in Corinth, Galatia, and especially in Ephesus, illustrate the relentlessness of the assault on community. Despite their access to divine directives and, in the case of the Jerusalem church, to the direct empowering of Pentecost, those congregations had to struggle fiercely to maintain their identities as community. Today, this onslaught on community seems to have escalated worldwide into a fight to the finish.

The family unit, regarded as the basic bastion of stability in most cultures, is disintegrating in many parts of the world under the burden of poverty and migrations of people from arid rural areas to monstrously overpopulated, slum-spawning megalopolises. In industrially developed countries, families are exploding serially under the pressures of modern life as they succumb to divorce, child neglect, domestic abuse, moral relativism, materialism, and the loss of ideals.

Schools and neighborhoods that were once safe and pleasant environments are festering with crime, rape, and substance abuse. Cities made to adorn the landscape of nations like jewels in a showcase are darkened with pollution, homelessness, unemployment, ghetto blight, the proliferation of firearms, and gang warfare. Nations destined to be proud and beautiful communities are often struggling for survival, engulfed in tidal waves of violence, tribal warfare, chaotic economies, shattered values, and media disorientation.

The ebb and flow of waves of uprooted refugees and the mass migration of whole populations of displaced persons were once the dreadful results of war. Now they have become the tragic routines of peace as millions wander about across continents and on treacherous seas in quest of food, employment, and security. Even during rare periods of global peace, one can safely wager that, whenever these lines will be read in the future, there will be a score of ethno-religious armed conflicts being waged in various parts of the world, sometimes even within culturally and economically advanced countries.

Modern knowledge and futuristic technologies have the capacity to resolve practically every demographic or economic problem on the face of the earth. Yet relational and social distress in multiple forms has reached a magnitude never attained before in the history of humankind. Wherever it still exists, community is under siege.

In order to protect itself against the onslaught of such anti-community forces, society comes up with institutions devised to hold the social fabric together: government, business, schools, technology, capitalism, socialism, market economics, the welfare state, and a dozen ideologies that claim the power to build community. But at the end of the twentieth century, a sentiment of fatigue and despair prevails, as if all the solutions have been tried and, instead of a new world order emerging, the problems are becoming more complex, the conflicts more inextricable, and the ideals of community more elusive than ever.

In the midst of this turmoil, Christians sense that the church holds the potential to provide solutions. We believe in a God who moves redemptively in our lives and who, therefore, has the power to effect change in the world. So, we pray to him, "Your kingdom come, your will be done on earth as it is in heaven." We believe in fulfilling the great commission that Christ laid upon his followers to make disciples of all nations, and many of us strive personally to obey it. We know we are called to be salt and light to this unsavory and darkened world. We also know that our influence is supposed to spread through society like the pervasive effect of a small piece of yeast that a woman mixes in a tub of flour to permeate and leaven the whole dough. Above all, we as Christians serve a living Christ who claimed, in reference to the opposition, that "the ruler of this world will be driven out. And I, when I am lifted up from the earth, will draw all people to myself" (John 12:31–32 NRSV).

Such high expectations only increase the sense of dismay and frustration of thoughtful Christians at our powerlessness to bring about change. Instead of Satan being driven out, we see the church being driven out of consideration in a world to which it is called to minister. And as far as Christ drawing all people to himself, church leaders consider themselves fortunate if they can keep their own members and their young people instead of losing them to the opposition. Too often, the church seems to be fighting a losing battle for its own survival when it should be the prevailing church, a force unleashed to crush the gates of hell.

An increasing number of Christians are waking up to the fact that, to a large extent, the church has become ineffective in fulfilling its mission because it has lost a sense of its own identity as community. They realize that not every organization that calls itself a church represents the church as Christ conceived it. As a result, we observe, toward the end of the second millennium of the life of the church, the emergence of a "community movement." This fact alone should give one pause. Such a sign of the need of the church for a reminder of its fundamental *raison d'être* gives a measure of the rot that has set in at the very core of its existence. Whereas the essential definition of the church is to be the community of oneness that unites God's people into one body, the church, after twenty centuries of existence, has to rediscover its own basic identity as community. As commendable as it is, this quest for community within the contemporary church suggests how far the church has strayed from the intentions of its divine founder by failing to remain what it was designed to be.

Recently, I asked a class of fifty junior and senior college students, all of them raised in church-going families, to write a one sentence definition of the church. Their answers varied from "people who are saved" and "places of worship" to "opportunity to put on a Sunday disguise" and "sanctified gossip centers." Not a single student described the church in terms of community or oneness. It occurred to me that such young people had been nurtured in the church without ever understanding the nature of their experience. The church was for them a habit without definition. They had been trained to play church or to do church instead of *being* the church. Is it any wonder that they, like their parents before them, perpetuate the survival of floundering, self-absorbed, defensive, stagnant, if not regressive pseudo-churches, thinking all along that they are doing God's work? Is it any wonder that the world should dismiss the church as irrelevant, treat it as a laughingstock, and view it as a farce instead of a force?

When he ordained his followers to be salt and light in this world, Christ expected the fellowship they would form to become a distinctive community that would serve as a model for the world. This would require that Christians be different not only in their individual lifestyles but also in the way they relate to each other. Therefore, Jesus expressly and severely forbade his followers to structure their communities according to patterns borrowed from the secular world (Matt. 20:25–28). The only model they were allowed to follow was the interrelationships of oneness within the Trinity (John 17:11, 20–22). Because oneness is the sole option prescribed by God for the structuring of relationships among adults in church and family, believers are forbidden to conform their communities to the patterns of this world. They must be transformed by the renewing of their mind (Rom. 12:1–2) in accordance with God's ideal for community.

During the first centuries of its history, the church managed to live and develop according to the design laid out by its divine founder. It was essentially a people's movement, whose members were bonded together by an intense loyalty to each other in communities governed by the ideals of mutuality and reciprocal servanthood. But things began to deteriorate in the fourth century with the alleged conversion of the Roman emperor Constantine. Christianity was made the official state religion, with the result that the church turned imperial and institutional. During the Middle Ages, therefore, the church assumed the form of an authoritarian organization ruled by clergy who grudgingly dispensed salvation to the faithful in order to secure their allegiance. Instead of acting as the transforming community, the church had conformed to the dominant anti-community model of the time.

A tidal wave of change swept over the church during the sixteenth century in the Protestant Reformation. The recognition of the freedom of inquiry and of the right to private interpretation released believers from the crushing oppression of the institutional church. But this emphasis on individual accountability to God, combined with the eighteenth-century deification of reason as the supreme judge of truth during the Enlightenment, contributed to the fragmentation of the church into a multitude of splinter groups, as if every individual were a church unto oneself. Thus were spawned endlessly denominations and sub-denominations that did not recognize each other, often competed against each other, and, too often, fought each other.

So much for the oneness of the church! Because of its refusal to pattern itself on the model of oneness provided by the Trinity, the church now vacillates between the worldly extreme of oppressive institutionalism on one hand and radical individualism on the other; that is, massive totalitarianism or frenzied fragmentation. In either case, the church fails to model and to provide community on behalf of God to a world deprived of it and yearning for it. Instead of the world being challenged and transformed by the newness of God-like community, it is the church that conforms to the anti-community patterns of the world.

To a certain extent, the failure of the church to stand for authentic community was predictable. As noted in chapter 1, the first reported casualty of Satan's attack in the Garden of Eden was community. Sin wrenched the man and the woman apart so that they faced each other no longer as one but as rivals. As God attempted to reintroduce community through the old covenant, it came under massive and repeated attacks. It was inevitable that the church, the new covenant community, would also become the favorite target of the evil one's attacks.

In the Old Testament this evil one is appropriately called "Satan," which means "adversary," "enemy." In the New Testament, he receives a new name, "the devil," which comes from the Greek word *diaballo*, which means "to throw apart." That is precisely what the devil does best: to separate and to divide, to destroy community. Having irreversibly separated himself from God, Satan becomes the sinister perpetrator of separation. What God unites, he divides; what God gathers, he scatters.

Jesus foresaw this attack and prepared his disciples to face it. He compared the church to a flock that would come under attack from a thief, who comes only to steal, kill, and destroy, and from a wolf, which snatches the sheep and scatters them (John 10:10, 12). But our Lord also assured them that, despite assaults from devilish anti-community forces, the gates of hell would not prevail against the church (Matt. 16:18). To his beleaguered followers he left this promise: "Do not be afraid, little flock, for your Father has been pleased to give you the kingdom" (Luke 12:32). Ultimately, the new community will prevail, and the gates of hell will be crushed.

But for this to happen, the church must be willing to search its conscience, to examine its beliefs and practices in the light of Scriptures, and to reform itself under the guidance of the Holy Spirit whenever necessary. The church must realize that the gates of hell are relentlessly striving to prevail against it.

As a legacy of the Fall, the weakest point in the defense system of the church against the attacks of hell is its practice of community. Because it is not of the world, the church is vulnerable to many dangers, such as pagan opposition, persecution, false teaching, apostasy, ungodly leadership, spiritual apathy, and conformity to secular ideologies and lifestyles. But the greatest of these is lack of love and the resulting breakdown of community. A church unable to live out its definition as community becomes the defenseless target of everything the opposition has to throw at it. On the other hand, a church intentionally committed to nurture and protect its life as community of oneness develops a God-given defense system that shields it against the destructive anti-community devices of the enemy.

Christians must always remember that not even Eden was evil-proof. The first loss ever incurred by humankind occurred as Satan found his way in the garden and, by causing sin to happen, shattered community. Ever since, the shattering of community has remained his favorite activity. Oneness is the most precious commodity present among humans, since it reflects the very nature of God, but it is also the most vulnerable and the most fragile.

The ease with which relational breakdowns occur bears witness to the vulnerability of community. Not even Christian communities, be they church or family, are spared such breakdowns. Churches may manage to exist without the oneness that should be their distinctive characteristic. But deprived of the heartbeat of authentic community, they can only muddle along as pseudo-churches, bereft of the vitality and power that would normally be available to them as expressions of God's community of oneness.

B. COMMITMENT TO COMMUNITY:
SMALL GROUPS

For a church to develop and maintain oneness is not a take-it-or-leave-it option. It is a priority and a mandate. Just as oneness was God's intention in creation (Gen. 2:24), it became God's creation in redemption. The making of oneness was Christ's overwhelming burden during his priestly prayer on behalf of the church just prior to his death (John 17:11, 21–23).

As the answer to Christ's prayer in the Upper Room, oneness happened naturally under the fresh impact of the Holy Spirit on Christ's followers at Pentecost: "All the believers were one in heart and mind" (Acts 4:32). But as the effect of that impact wore off and Christians increasingly took for granted both the Holy Spirit and their oneness, the churches had to be constantly reminded of their true identity as the communities of oneness.

Writing to the Christians of Rome, the apostle Paul insisted that "in Christ we who are many form one body, and each member belongs to all the others" (Rom. 12:5). The Christians in Corinth needed to be told that, because they were all in communion with the same Christ represented by one loaf at the Lord's Supper, they were all one body, although many members (1 Cor. 10:17). Paul also wrote to them, "You are the body of Christ, and each one of you is a part of it" (12:27). His explanation for the mystery of this oneness was the uniting power of the Holy Spirit that had been granted to the church as of the day of Pentecost: "We were all baptized by one Spirit into one body—whether Jews or Greeks, slaves or free—and we were all given the one Spirit to drink" (v. 13).

To the churches in Galatia, tempted to adopt legalistic and discriminating distinctions, Paul emphatically declared, "There is neither Jew nor Greek, slave nor free, male nor female, for you are all one in Christ Jesus" (Gal. 3:28). The same danger threatened other churches, where some Christians wanted to segregate people on the basis of their racial backgrounds as Gentiles and Jews. So, Paul told them, in the church Christ "made both groups into one and has broken down the dividing wall ... that he might create in himself a new humanity in the place of the two ... and might reconcile both groups to God in one body through the cross" (Eph. 2:14–16 NRSV). As a result, "There is one body and one Spirit—just as you were called to one hope when you were called—one Lord, one faith, one baptism, one God and Father of all, who is over all and through all and in all" (4:4–6).

Paul expressed the same concern for oneness to the church that was dearest to him. He encouraged the Philippian Christians to stand "firm in one spirit, striving side by side with one mind for the faith of the gospel" (Phil. 1:27 NRSV) and to be "one in spirit and purpose" (2:2). On another occasion, he wrote to the Colossians to remind them that they were "members of one body" (Col. 3:15) because "Christ is all, and is in all" (v. 11).

This brief survey of the importance of oneness for the church reveals that, according to the New Testament, oneness is like salvation. It is a divine gift to humans, but it has to be appropriated by them in order to become a reality in their lives. The practical implementation of relationships of oneness within the structures of ministry and leadership will be discussed in the following chapters. In the meantime, it should become obvious that the primary application of the biblical mandate for communal life can only take place in a context of closeness and togetherness. Necessarily, this spells "small groups."

In the experience of many people, church is reduced to attendance at a service on Sunday morning. This is not really church. The Sunday morning hour is essentially an experience of corporate worship. As important as worship is for the welfare of the church, it represents only one aspect of its life. Sitting in rows or pews and looking at each other's backs for one hour per week can hardly be described as communal life.

The biblical metaphor of "family" more appropriately describes what the church should resemble—a group of people, few enough in numbers to sit around in a circle, facing each other and sharing the joy and the benefits of togetherness. Every church that aspires to function as community must make a small group structure available to its constituency. The alternative is to shrink to the status of a Sunday morning worship station. A congregation that comprises more than fifty adults is too large to function as community—unless it is organized in small groups where communal life can thrive.

It is in small groups that people can get close enough to know each other, to care and share, to challenge and support, to confide and confess, to forgive and be forgiven, to laugh and weep together, to be accountable to each other, to watch over each other, and to grow together. Personal growth does not happen in isolation. It is the result of interactive relationships. Small groups are God's gift to foster changes in character and spiritual growth.

Jesus had many followers, but he chose from among them a small group of twelve, and then he formed from among the twelve an even smaller group of four, including himself. This smaller small group surrounded Jesus, in total or in part, at critical points in his ministry (Matt. 17:1; Mark 5:37; 14:33; John 13:23; 18:15; 20:2; 21:7, 20). When he sent the disciples as short-term missionaries, he was careful that they would not go alone but two by two (Mark 6:7). He even made sure that they would not go alone for lesser errands (11:1; 14:13). He emphasized the effectiveness of small group prayers (Matt. 18:19), and he promised that when two or three people would gather as a small group—surprise!—he would be there with them (v. 20). Obviously, Jesus loves small groups. He, with the Father and the Spirit, formed the original and quintessential small group.

On Pentecost Day, Jesus sent the Holy Spirit to form the church (Acts 2:1–4). He just could not let his followers remain in a state of noncommunity. For those first Christians, fellowshiping together became a priority, second only to the preaching of the Word (v. 42). In many churches today, the preaching of the Word has become a substitute for communal life. People gather on Sunday morning to listen to a sermon and they call that "fellowship." But preaching and fellowship are two distinct features of the life of the church.

Although the first Christians loved to gather in a large group at the temple for corporate worship, they also met in small groups. In fact, they enjoyed so much being in small groups that they assembled every day. And then, they were so happy together that they could not break away from each other. So they stayed and had their meals together (Acts 2:46). Later, when Christianity reached the great metropolises of the time, believers continued to experience community in the context of home churches (Rom. 16:5, 10, 11, 14–15; 1 Cor. 16:15, 19, etc.). Today, wherever the church thrives as community, even in those parts of the world where it suffers under persecution, it is without fail structured on the basis of small groups.

For contemporary Christians, to meet regularly in small groups is not an option or a luxury. It is a biblical mandate that they must obey if they want to experience communal life and if their churches are to become biblically functioning communities. Whenever church leadership is slow or reluctant to get a small group structure in place as a regular part of its program, laypeople have every right to get together and form their own small groups. Such a vast amount of literature and aids on small group organization and small group leadership training is available today that no one needs to feel without resources in facing this exciting challenge.

C. THE HAZARDS OF COMMUNITY

If the Scriptures provide helpful prescriptions for the welfare of the church as community, they also identify the dangers that threaten community and hinder its development. We now turn to two of these hindrances

1. The Mutilation of the Cross

A correlation was made above between the physical shape of the cross and the two great commandments of Scripture (page 33). The response of obedience to the commandment to love God "with all your heart and with all your soul and with all your mind" is made possible by the reconciliation that Christ has effected between God and humans through his death on the cross. This relation is symbolized by the vertical trunk of the cross. Through it, God above finds us in our sinfulness below and offers us his salvation. Redemption is primarily a personal transaction that occurs at the individual level. Each person is accountable to respond to God's offer of salvation with repentance and faith in him, thus establishing a personal relationship with him.

But the cross has also a horizontal dimension, which corresponds to the second greatest commandment, to love our neighbor as ourselves. Christ died not only for you as an individual but also for others. Through the outstretched arms of the cross, he gathers together to himself, in the community of reconciliation and oneness, all those who seek reconciliation with God (Eph. 2:14–16).

Obviously, there could have been no cross if either one of its segments had been missing. As important as the vertical trunk is, it also requires the horizontal beam. Likewise, without the support of the vertical stem, the crossbar collapses into nothingness. In other words, individual salvation and community integration cannot be separated. One without the other causes the cross to lose its redemptive power. The Scripture clearly teaches that there can be no love of God that is genuine without it resulting in the love of others (1 John 3:10, 14–18). Conversely, love for neighbor apart from the love of God has no redemptive value (1 Cor. 16:22). The two great commandments are inextricably interdependent, as are the two parts of the cross.

Tragically, many Christians act as enemies of the cross by taking it apart and discarding one of its two elements. Some emphasize exclusively the blessing of individual salvation and the need for a personal relationship with God through Christ. They devote themselves to cultivating their spiritual life through prayer, Bible study, meditation, writing journals, and various spiritual disciplines in vogue at the moment. But they have no corresponding interest in extending themselves to others in need and thus fulfilling the law of love by serving them sacrificially. They selfishly exalt the vertical dimension of the cross but trample underfoot the equally important horizontal requirement of love. Their religion degenerates into fruitless, egocentric, consumer-oriented spiritual narcissism.

Others engage in a flurry of social activism by taking up any cause that calls for protests, demonstrations, and intervention. They care for the poor, the oppressed and the helpless—as well they should! They carefully tend their friendships and cultivate family relationships. But they neglect the personal dimension of faith. Many such well-doers are unable to profess whether they have made a personal commitment of faith to God. The work they do is valuable, but unbelievers could do as much. It is not empowered by the motivation of love for God and a desire to serve him.

There is much truth up and down the vertical dimension of the cross, just as there is much truth all along its horizontal dimension. But our identity as Christians is to be found at the intersection of both dimensions. That is the center where we all belong. This point of convergence is attained when we obey both great commandments and neglect neither. Obedient Christians find their oneness by meeting at the focal point of the cross. The community of oneness is not achieved by Christians who love God or by Christians who love their neighbor. It is achieved by Christians who love God *and* their neighbor. By so doing, they come together at the center of the cross and discover their only place of oneness.

In this regard, one of the most important but often ignored statements of Scripture is found in Romans 15:7. In the context, Paul invokes for his readers "a spirit of unity" so that they may be able to worship "with one heart and mouth" (vv. 5–6). The text itself is a terse, practical command intended to facilitate the implementation of this community of oneness: "Accept one another, then, just as Christ has accepted you, in order to bring praise to God" (v. 7).

This scriptural imperative cuts across all the complexities of life, the intricacies of relationships, and the difficulties of building community. It goes to the core of the issue of oneness. It tells us that oneness is achieved when we meet at the center of the cross, where its two parts intersect. The command requires us to "accept one another"—the horizontal dimension of love—as "Christ accepted" us—the vertical dimension of God's love for us. Therein lies the secret of the workings of oneness. Christ's acceptance of us is gracious, total, unreserved, unprejudiced, forgiving, and freeing. So should be our acceptance of each other.

This prescription for oneness forbids Christians intent on building community to construct it around worldly considerations of rank, status, gender, race, fortune, or social standing. Christ does not take into account such factors for his acceptance of believers, nor should his followers. In order to become true oneness, community is to be built by people who accept each other as Christ accepts them.

The only exception allowed in Scripture to this rule is the distinction between the "weak" and the "strong," the unspiritual believer and the mature Christian. But even here, the strong are to help the weak become strong, because this is precisely what Christ did for us when he took abuse instead of seeking his own interest (Rom. 15:1–3). Biblical oneness happens at the intersection of Christ's acceptance of us and of our acceptance of each other. Then Paul goes on to add that this reflection in relationships among Christians of Christ's love toward us is what brings glory to God (v. 7). The supreme act of worship is to strive for biblical oneness.

How does Christ accept you? Does he ask what race you belong to, whether you are rich or poor, smart or stupid, man or woman, married, single, or divorced? In the words of Scripture, does he ask whether you are Jew or Gentile, slave or free, male or female, circumcised or uncircumcised, barbarian or Scythian? Absolutely not! The only question Jesus asks is whether you want to receive his love. There is no other question because at the foot of the cross the ground is level, and at its center, there is no room but for oneness.

By what right, then, do we turn around and ask of each other additional questions—hellish questions that discriminate, demean, divide, and destroy? By what right do we dismember the cross and replace it with our worldly hierarchies of upward mobility: clergy at the top, laity below; white Caucasians at the top, "minorities" below; men at the top, women below; the rich at the top, the "losers" below; the educated at the top, the simpleminded below; the ordained at the top, the congregation below; leaders at the top, followers below? Didn't Christ grab in his mighty hands those damnable ladders of stratification, turn them upside down, and crush them into the shape of a cross? Didn't he himself set the example of downward mobility for those who strive to be first and great (cf. Mark 10:41–45)? Didn't he command them to be last and least in order to find their proper place in the oneness of his community?

A sobering passage of Scripture compares the oneness of the church to the temple of God, the dwelling place of his Spirit. It contains a most severe warning against those who would destroy the church by sowing the seeds of division and discrimination among Christians: "If anyone destroys God's temple, God will destroy him; for God's temple is sacred, and you are that temple" (1 Cor. 3:17). It is no trifling matter to divide what God unites. It perpetuates the dirty work of Satan in the Garden. It's as if one were striking at God himself. He protects oneness because he is oneness.

God loves human oneness because of the God-likeness of oneness. He hates divisions because they are the work of the enemy. Oneness has beauty and goodness, simplicity and nobility. Hierarchies, which divide and emphasize differences instead of pulling people together, are ugly. For this reason, the Scriptures declare that faith in the Lord Jesus Christ and favoritism are incompatible. Partiality violates the Lord of glory (James 2:1). To elevate some people by putting others down is to discriminate. Before God, such discriminations are no better than the decisions of a corrupt judge who lets the evil one control his thinking (v. 4). To practice favoritism in the community is a sin that makes the perpetrator of discrimination liable to conviction, as if the whole law of God had been broken and murder committed (vv. 8–11).

When referring to the manner of his death, Jesus attributed to the cross the power to draw all humanity together into oneness. He claimed: "When I am lifted up from the earth, I will draw all people to myself" (John 12:32 NRSV). God will not allow the cross, his instrument for the re-creation of oneness, to be dismantled with impunity. God expects us to accept one another without partiality, prejudice, or discrimination, and to treat each other with love as equals, as evenhandedly as Christ himself deals with us.

2. The Shrinking of Sanctification

An even more subtle hindrance to the creation of oneness stems from a faulty understanding of the biblical doctrine of sanctification. The Scriptures make it clear that sanctification is an essential process of growth in the life of believers: "This is the will of God, your sanctification" (1 Thess. 4:3 NRSV). Sanctification is usually understood as the activity of the Holy Spirit within believers to restore the image of God that was disrupted by the Fall. It follows, then, that the purpose of sanctification is to develop Christ-likeness in character and behavior within each believer.

While absolutely correct, this definition of sanctification all too easily emphasizes exclusively the individual dimension of the work of the Spirit within each believer. It misses the fuller implications of the restoration of the image of God in human life.

There is a lot more to the restoration of the image of God in human life than the cultivation of personal holiness as a private spiritual exercise. In the beginning, the image of God had a relational dimension (see chap. 1). The nature of the Godhead as a plurality of interdependent persons provided the model for relationships among humans. It was not good for the man to be alone because his creation in God's image called for a union of oneness with someone like him. Soon after the creation of human oneness, this interrelational dimension of God's image became the first casualty of the Fall, with the destruction of community. And in God's program of redemption, it becomes the first focus of sanctification.

The Scriptures describe sanctification as the replacement of the self principle in human life by the Spirit principle (Rom. 8:9). The self principle causes us to do as we please in order to please ourselves; the Spirit principle prompts us to do the will of God in order to please him (v. 5; Gal. 5:17). Predictably, living according to the self principle results in alienation, relational breakdowns, and social chaos. Living according to the Spirit principle leads to relational harmony and community building.

This polarity is starkly described in a well-known section of Scripture, Galatians 5:16–26. Activities derived from the self principle are obvious; they are predatory excesses that victimize others by using them for selfish gratification. These are listed as sexual immorality, impurity, and debauchery (v. 19); perversions of worship, such as idolatry and witchcraft (v. 20, interest in the occult being one expression of idolatry and greed another; cf.

Eph. 5:5); relational dysfunctions, such as hatred, discord, jeal-ousy, fits of rage, selfish ambition, dissensions, factions, and envy (Gal. 5:20–21); and, finally, self-indulgent, addictive behaviors, such as drunkenness and orgies (v. 21). Living according to the self principle is always detrimental to individuals who choose to go that way; but, even more so, it has destructive effects on the social environments of which they are a part.

Submitting to the Spirit principle, on the other hand, has the opposite effect. The sanctifying impact of the Holy Spirit pro-duces attitudes and behaviors that not only enhance individual personhood, but also provide the basic elements for stable and harmonious community life. Each of the elements listed as the "fruit" or the result of the activity of the Spirit in a person's life has a relational frame of reference: love, joy, peace, patience, kindness, goodness, faithfulness, gentleness, and self-control (Gal. 5:22–23). Each one of these characteristics of the fruit of the Spirit presupposes contexts of relationships with other per-sons for its expression.

In other words, sanctification cannot be achieved in isolation. It is a community-sustained and directed endeavor. God's law condemns the self principle because of its anti-community effects. But no such restriction has been attached to "the fruit of the Spirit" (v. 23). There is no law against it because its results conform to the nature of God by generating oneness.

A faulty understanding of sanctification as a self-absorbed, pri-vate exercise of personal improvement has a fragmenting effect on the church. It must be replaced with a vigorous, holistic doc-trine of sanctification that defines it also as the God-given spiri-tual cement that makes oneness possible.

It should be noted in this regard that the Scripture's definition of the "fruit of the Spirit" as personhood remade in the image of God has poignant relevance for contemporary Christian men and women. Recent years have seen the emergence of "women's movements," which call on women to contend for equal power and equal rights. Such programs clash with ideals of Christian community building. Relationships of oneness are not based on competition for power or rights, but, to the contrary, on biblically prescribed attitudes of mutual submission and reciprocal servanthood (Matt. 20:26–27; Rom. 15:1–2; Gal. 5:13–14; Eph. 5:21; Phil. 2:1–5; etc.).

The contemporary "men's movements" do not seem to fare much better—even when they are promoted by Christian leaders. When Christian men are called upon to uphold their spiritual commitments, many of them interpret this challenge as a license to assert their masculinity as, unhappily, it has been traditionally understood in our culture. A religious leader who claims to be an authority on family issues reportedly greeted thousands of men at a recent rally as "hairy-chested, testosterone-driven males," while declaring that "women are incurable romantics." Instead of mouthing pagan stereotypes, the speaker would have been better advised to challenge the men to become Christ-like, to develop the fruit of the Spirit, and to cultivate servanthood in a structure of accountability to their wives and not just to other men.

According to Scriptures, there are not two kinds of spirituality, one for men, the other for women. The model is the same for both: Jesus Christ. He exemplifies to perfection the profile of a personality that incarnates the "fruit of the Spirit." Our culture generally defines "real manhood" as being tough, driven, aggressive, expeditious, forceful, opportunistic, competitive, and self-indulgent. To make matters worse, many women who think they must strive for equality with men adopt the same standards. However, the norms both for biblical manhood and for biblical womanhood are diametrically opposed to the cultural definitions of "real manhood." They are exactly the same for both men and women: "love, joy, peace, patience, kindness, goodness, faithfulness, gentleness and self-control," the natural expressions of relationships within structures of mutual submission and servanthood (Gal. 5:22; cf. 5:13; Eph. 5:21).

Modern men and women are immersed in a world tragically deprived of oneness. Wherever they turn, whether in the domain of business, government, politics, education, employment, the military, or domestic life, they come up against non-community systems of hierarchy, stratification, and competition that divide and isolate. Yet, because they are made in the image of God, who is oneness, they yearn to belong, to be loved, and to experience as adults the warm security of human oneness. To the church belongs the privileged opportunity to offer them the gift of oneness on God's behalf.

To this end, the church faces two options. It can either choose the model of mutual submission and servanthood that God established at the beginning, or it can adopt the patterns of dominance and rulership that derived from the Fall. When the church becomes worldly and replaces oneness with hierarchy and sanctification with stratification, modern pagans find no reason to trade one form of hell for another. The church is called to be the radically different community of oneness that embodies the divine alternative to the world.

CHAPTER THREE

Ministry

As exciting as the ideal of community is, it does not happen by itself. To establish authentic community and to make it work properly requires forethought, organization, coordination, and cooperation. Biblically, all the work that building community requires is called "ministry." Unfortunately, in popular parlance, ministry is something that is done by special people called "ministers" or "priests." The problem with this interpretation of ministry is that it excludes most of the members of the community from being significantly involved in building it. Therefore, it is once again necessary to examine closely the teachings of the Bible on this subject to determine from Scripture what ministry is, how it is to be done, and by whom.

A. MINISTRY IN THE BEGINNING

Historically, ministry began with the stewardship responsibilities that God assigned to Adam and Eve in the garden. At the very beginning, when Adam was by himself, God put him in the garden "to work it and take care of it" (Gen. 2:15). It would have been within the capacity of a sovereign God to create a maintenance-free environment so that Adam could have spent his days in total leisure, lounging on beds of ease and enjoying in happy idleness the natural beauty that surrounded him. But God, who is a worker-creator and who has a servant heart, formed the human being in his image so that he would also enjoy working as God's servant.

Human community began when Eve was created. The growth potential of this community required the assignment of increased responsibilities. Now, it was no longer enough for Adam just to tend the garden. Because there were two of them with many more to follow, the extent of their stewardship was redefined and greatly expanded. The man and the woman were commanded together to subdue the earth and to "rule over the fish of the sea and the birds of the air and over every living creature that moves on the ground" (Gen. 1:28). This considerable enterprise was committed to them as a blessing, not as a punishing chore; it was their ministry. God entrusted them with such a high level of authority because he loved them as his image-bearers and respected the stewardship potential he had invested in them.

The Scripture does not specify how Adam and Eve were supposed to organize themselves to accomplish their tasks. The only thing that the text reveals is that God made them both rulers over the earth. But since they were also God's servants, they brought to the task their best stewardship, each one contributing from his and from her own ability to the success of their partnership. They were at work together, neither one being sidelined while the other did ministry.

God entrusted the pair with an additional responsibility: "Be fruitful and multiply, and fill the earth" (1:28 NRSV). That is, they were also supposed to populate the earth in order to expand community. Obviously, the woman was the childbearer. But there is a lot more to having children and raising them than just giving birth. Significantly, God entrusted this task to both of them because it was to be their joint ministry. Neither one was excused or excluded from it.

At least three lessons may be drawn about the nature of ministry from the story of the beginnings. First, in the divine order of things, the making of community requires work. Community does not just happen. Second, the members of community are servants together under divine authority. They are all "ministers"—a term derived from a Latin word that means "servant." Third, the work of community requires the total involvement of its members. No one is excluded or excused from contributing, out of one's abilities, to the common tasks.

This was community as God had intended it to function forever—a self-perpetuating, self-maintaining collectivity made of harmonious, mutually-deferential servant relationships, where each one brought to the group his or her best contribution. Had God's will for community prevailed, this would have been the whole story for human history. The Bible would have been a very short book—the first two chapters of Genesis with perhaps a tiny concluding third chapter to confirm that everything was fine in the best possible of all worlds, because everyone was submitted to God and to each other, and that they all lived happily together ever after.

B. MINISTRY: A PRIVILEGE FOR THE FEW

Unfortunately, we know things turned out differently. The human uprising against God that we call "the Fall" wreaked havoc on the neat arrangement God had implanted in the Garden of Eden. God's design for ministry as participatory stewardship was turned on its head by the entrance of sin on the human scene. Whereas a servant-to-servant relationship had originally prevailed among humans, the Fall brought about a ruler-servant relationship (Gen. 3:16). Within such a structure of hierarchy, participation in communal tasks became subject to the will of the individual holding authority over the community.

In addition to this degradation of God's design for community, the ministries originally entrusted by God to the humans turned from blessing to curse. Instead of conveying God's blessing as originally intended (1:28), childbearing became painful labor for the woman, and subduing the earth became hard labor for the man (3:16–19). Ministry tasks that were intended to be carried out corporately (1:28) became separated into predetermined roles for the woman and the man. Because of human sin, communal stewardship gave way to separation and exclusion.

After the Fall, God had every right to call it quits on his human community project and to pull the plug on history. Instead, the loving, servant heart of God devised a plan for the reclamation of his creation. The plan began with the old covenant, a time of preparation for the coming of Christ and for the beginning of the church. This proved to be a period of frustration. Although some positive signs of what God wanted to do in the new community were present, to a great extent the negative effects of the Fall prevailed during that time. Such hindrances would be removed only through the redemptive ministry of Jesus Christ (see Bilezikian, *Beyond Sex Roles,* pp. 59–78).

God had promised the old covenant people that, if they would only remain faithful to him, he would make of them a kingdom of priests (Ex. 19:5–6). In God's dream, every member of his community would function like a priest, and he alone would be their king. Everyone would be a minister and God would be their benevolent ruler.

However, because of the lack of cooperation from the people, things did not turn out the way God had wanted them to go. Ministry became the privilege of a few "ruler"-type individuals, while the majority of the people remained on the outside looking in. Gradually, three categories of people emerged as ministry specialists on behalf of the people—priests, prophets, and kings.

The priests were recruited from one of the twelve Hebrew tribes. They represented a minority drawn from a minority. They were attached to the service of the tabernacle and, later, of the temple that replaced it. Their function was to minister in worship before God and to offer sacrifices on behalf of the people. As such, they eventually acquired a special status of authority and influence over and among the people whom they had been appointed to serve.

The prophets were men and women who were called from all walks of life to speak God's word to the people in times of need and in situations of crisis. Unlike the priests, they did not constitute an upper class among the people. Their service was ad hoc and generally not hereditary. They were the recognized dispensers of God's message to the people.

The real king of the people was God himself; they were his kingdom. God tried to protect the people from falling subject to a monarchic authority structure as long as he could. But the people became increasingly rebellious and wicked as they replaced communal life with confusion: "Every one did as he saw fit" (Judg. 21:25). Their calling was to be a nation of priests and to serve each other (Ex. 19:6). Instead, they all started doing their own thing and looking after their own interests.

As a result, in order to bring some order in the midst of this frenzy of individualism run amuck (not unlike our own times), God sent "judges." They were men and women called from all walks of life who attempted to bring the people to reason—but in vain. Then, to add insult to injury, the people demanded a king, and they got what they wanted. As such, kings were usurpers because the real king was supposed to be God. So the monarchy was established in violation of God's will and with disastrous consequences for the people (1 Sam. 8:7; 10:19; 12:19; etc.).

Reluctantly but graciously, God accepted the monarchic system in anticipation of the advent of the supreme King, the Messiah, whom he was planning to send into the world. The Messiah would be the one to bring to fulfillment God's dream of a people who would truly be a "royal priesthood" (1 Peter 2:9, cf. v. 5). With him as King, God would finally be sole ruler of the church, his new community.

C. MINISTRY: A RESPONSIBILITY FOR ALL

With the advent of Christ, the predicted change from old covenant to new community took place. Once he had committed his teaching to his followers and after he was crucified, buried, and raised to life again, he sent the Holy Spirit to get the church started. This great release of divine power into the outflow of history had a profound effect on the three institutions of the old covenant. The priesthood, the prophetic function, and the kingly office as defined in the old covenant were radically affected through this paradigm shift.

1. A New Priesthood

The old covenant priests officiated in the temple by offering worship to God on behalf of the people. According to the New

Testament, the church as a people is now God's new temple, and all believers are his priests. Early in his ministry, Jesus predicted that he would rebuild the temple as his body through his death and resurrection (John 2:19–22). This body of Christ is God's sacred temple, his people within whom his Spirit lives (1 Cor. 3:16–17; 2 Cor. 6:16; Eph. 2:21–22).

In keeping with Old Testament imagery, God's people are the spiritual house where God's Spirit lives, and they are also the priests who serve within it. Like the ancient priests, their task is to offer "sacrifices acceptable to God" (1 Peter 2:5). But the sacrifices offered now by God's people are not animals slaughtered over an altar, as in the old covenant temple. They are infinitely more valuable and useful. Even more importantly, they also have the advantage of being offered by all of God's people—not just by a few privileged men among them—because now all believers have become priests unto God (Rom. 12:1). In actual practice, these sacrifices are of two kinds: worship (Heb. 13:15) and good deeds, especially sharing with the needy (v. 16). Such priestly service and such sacrifices are pleasing to God.

This expansion of the concept of priesthood into one that includes all Christians rather than a small coterie of privileged professionals transforms every believer into a minister. A minister is someone who does ministry. According to the New Testament, every believer is a minister (cf. Eph. 4:12). This concept should come as no surprise since all believers share a common oneness at the center of the cross and, therefore, have an equal stake in the outworking of that oneness (1 Cor. 12:14–20).

What is surprising is that, in defiance of this New Testament teaching about the priesthood of all believers, religious tradition has reduced the designation of "priest" or "minister" to a small group of men within the church. Not only are they given special status and, often, set above the congregation to that place where only Christ belongs as sovereign, but since they are the "ministers," it is assumed that ministry belongs to them exclusively. No system could have been better devised to sabotage the mission of the church.

The result of this pattern of ministry is what Greg Ogden, a Presbyterian leader and author of the best book on this subject, calls "split-level churches" (*The New Reformation*, Zondervan, 1992). The community of oneness is replaced by discriminative structures of ministry that reflect worldly stratification rather than the oneness Christ died to achieve.

Obviously, congregations need leadership, and, as we shall see in the next chapter, the New Testament defines clearly the nature of such leadership roles. Suffice it to say here that leadership that arrogates to itself the ministry belonging to others, leadership that claims a monopoly on spiritual gifting, and leadership that substitutes itself for the priesthood of all believers is not scripturally warranted and does not come from God. It is the result of either a faulty interpretation of the concept of leadership or of uncritical regression to Old Testament patterns of ministry. In either case, what is needed is a new reformation, a careful reexamination of our theory and practice of ministry in the light of New Testament teachings and with a willingness to recognize and discard unbiblical traditions that hinder and so easily entangle.

2. A People of Prophets

If the new community has no super-priests, what about prophets? In the old covenant community, a few individuals were called occasionally to proclaim a message from God to the people. Not surprisingly, the pattern of expansion that we traced from a few priests in the old covenant to the priesthood of all believers in the new community also prevails with regard to the ministry of prophecy.

In the very first pronouncement made on the day of Pentecost, Peter announced that, as a result of the new availability of the Spirit to all believers, everyone would have access to the ministry of prophecy. God solemnly confirmed that not only "your sons and daughters will prophesy," but also "my servants, both men and women . . . will prophesy" (Acts 2:17–18). In the New Testament, the word "prophecy" acquires a broad meaning. It becomes the umbrella term that covers any ministry of the spoken word that results in "edification and exhortation and consolation" (1 Cor. 14:3 NASB).

Because Christ is the living Word and because he commanded that his Word be preached and taught universally, the ministries of the spoken word were at the forefront of the work and growth of the church from its very beginning. The first activity to which the apostles devoted themselves after Pentecost was "teaching"—obviously the transmission to the newborn church of what Christ himself had taught them (Acts 2:42; see also John 14:25–26). Because the church's very existence depended on the Word of God, the ministries of the Word had a place of primacy in the early church. They were the foremost ministries offered by God (1 Cor. 12:28) and the primary gifts made available by Christ (Eph. 4:11). The work of "preaching and teaching" was especially regarded as being "worthy of double honor" (1 Tim. 5:17).

As the church grew and expanded through the ancient world, so did the number of prophets, preachers, and teachers of the Word. Jesus had commanded his original apostles to make disciples of all nations and to teach what he had committed to them (Matt. 28:19–20). Having begun with this core group, the teaching ministry of the church was then taken up by people like Stephen (Acts 6:8–11), Philip (one of the Seven), many other Christians—including Philip's four daughters, who prophesied (8:4–6; 11:20–21; 21:9)—Saul of Tarsus (9:20) and his companions, both Jews and Gentiles (13:1), and countless numbers of unnamed followers of Jesus, who propagated his message in their neighborhoods and throughout the world (13:49).

The ministry of the Word spread mightily within local churches in the ancient world. The strategy was to commit the apostles' message "to faithful people able to teach others as well" (2 Tim. 2:2 NRSV). But God's ultimate plan was for the Word to be so richly available within each congregation that each believer could contribute to this ministry. Paul encouraged all the Christians in Corinth to prophesy (1 Cor. 14:1, 5a, 26, 31, 39 NRSV). Any qualified man or woman could lead the congregation in worship by praying and prophesying, provided appropriate attire was worn for the occasion (11:4–5). The Word of God was to dwell so richly within congregations that all Christians were exhorted to "teach and admonish one another with all wisdom" (Col. 3:16). They were all expected to become knowledgeable enough to be "competent to instruct one another" (Rom. 15:14; cf. Heb. 5:12).

The mystery of the vitality of the church lies in the message of God's self-disclosure in his Word and in the story of the redemption achieved through his Son's death and resurrection. The apostles provided the first link in the transmission of that story and message. As a result, these now belong to every believer to pass on to others. For this reason, the church's vitality also lies in the total participation of its constituency in the witness and proclamation ministries of the community.

3. Only One Lord

The kingly office had played a major part in the history of the old covenant. This ministry also experienced a profound change with the advent of the new community and under the impact of Christ's instructions to the disciples.

Unlike the old covenant people, the new community does not have an earthly king. Christ is king, and his kingdom extends to all the realms where his rule is accepted and wherever God's will is done as it is in heaven. Despite the lowliness of the circumstances of his birth, Jesus was recognized as king, ruler, and Lord (Matt. 2:2, 6; Luke 2:11). At age thirty and to inaugurate his three-year earthly ministry, he came proclaiming the kingdom (Matt. 4:17). A good part of his teaching ministry was devoted to describing the nature, future, and entrance requirements of his kingdom. When he was sentenced, he was recognized a king and died as such (John 19:14, 19). After his resurrection, his followers acclaimed him as Lord (Acts 2:36).

Because Christ is Lord and because the church is an expression of his kingdom, the church does not need an earthly ruler. The Lord in heaven is perfectly capable of managing the affairs of his church on earth, especially since the Holy Spirit is on location to attend to it. It is indeed the calling of every member of Christ's community to minister on the basis of one's gifts and talents. But it is no one's calling to act as mini-king or as superminister in Christ's church. The twelve apostles on one occasion were tempted to view themselves in such roles, but Jesus set them back sharply and showed them that acceptable stewardship in his kingdom meant servanthood and never competition for rulership or positions of authority (Matt. 20:20–28).

4. Jewish Male Apostles

An accurate understanding of the role of the twelve disciples during the ministry of Jesus is essential for a proper understanding of ministry in the church, especially in view of the fact that this group chosen by Jesus was exclusively comprised of Jewish males.

Apart from the Twelve, Jesus had many followers who were actively involved in ministry with and around him. Among them were the seventy-two missionaries who spoke and healed on his behalf (Luke 10:1–20) and a group of women who traveled with him and the Twelve (8:1–3). Among all of these, Jesus intentionally selected a group of twelve men as his disciples (students), in order to make them his apostles (missionaries). To the Twelve he committed his teaching, and he commanded them to pass it on after his ascension in order to make disciples of all the nations (Matt. 28:19). As such, the Twelve formed the nucleus that Christ would use to build his church, the new community (16:18).

The symbolism of the number twelve is self-evident. Jesus made clear a relation between the old covenant people represented by its twelve tribes and the people of the new community represented by the twelve apostles, with the latter taking precedence over the former (Luke 22:29–30). The ancient nation of Israel had begun with the patriarchs, the fathers of the twelve tribes. The new Israel, the spiritual descendants of Abraham, began with the twelve disciples. They were the new covenant counterpart to the twelve patriarchs. They formed the transition group between the past and the future, between the ancient people and the new community.

From the Twelve, the constituency of God's people was expanded to include followers of Christ from both the people of Israel and from all nations in order to form the universal church. The ultimate command of Jesus to the eleven remaining disciples was to make disciples of all the nations (Matt. 28:19). Their mission was to form a multitude of disciples like themselves. With the launching of that mission accomplished, they would fade into the multitude. In other words, they were to reproduce themselves as disciples so widely as to make their own ministry obsolete. According to the book of Acts and as is evident from the history of the early church, this is precisely what happened. The Twelve were the pioneer servant-ministers of the new community, and their lives eventually faded into anonymity.

As historically accurate as it is, the scenario described above raises a contradiction that should not be left unresolved. The mission of the Twelve was to lay the foundation for the establishment of a new community that would comprise men and women from all races and all ethnic groups. Yet the initial nucleus of this new community was not at all representative of its future constituency, for Jesus had pointedly chosen twelve Jewish men. In view of their prospective mission, it would seem to have been appropriate for Jesus to select a diversity of people, one that would reflect his intention for the composition of the new community. A typical mix would have included three Jewish men, three Jewish women, three Gentile men, and three Gentile women. Yet, Jesus deliberately selected a shockingly exclusive group of people—twelve male Jews—thus excluding both Gentiles and women.

At several points, the Gospels provide an explanation to this paradox, especially in that section where Jesus commissioned the Twelve by giving them his authority and sending them away to preach and heal (Matt. 10:1–8). The Gospel writer chose this precise point to interrupt the narrative and introduce formally each of the Twelve by name. The instructions that Jesus gave to the disciples for the conduct of their mission were then closely linked to the list of their names.

It comes as a shock that the first instruction about outreach given by Jesus to the newly commissioned disciples was one of sharp exclusion. He strictly forbade them to go among the Gentiles or to enter any town of the Samaritans (v. 5). Their ministry was to be strictly confined to Jewish people (v. 6).

The juxtaposition of the nominal identification of the Twelve with the prohibition for them to minister to anyone but Jews suggests that they had been selected by Jesus with this restricted mission in mind. Indeed, the narrative establishes a close connection between the identity of the twelve disciples and the boundaries of their immediate ministry. By linking the names of the disciples with Christ's command to minister to Jews only, the Gospel writer suggests that the disciples were chosen in function of this ministry. They were Jews who would first minister to Jews.

Obviously, this limited ministry of the Twelve was only intended as an interim phase of their life mission. It was a short-term outreach effort, contained within the time frame of the earthly ministry of Christ. Soon after this incident, Jesus described his mission as one of worldwide outreach (Matt. 13:37–38). And before his ascension, he recommissioned the same disciples to take the gospel to all the nations and, more pointedly, to carry their witness from Jerusalem and Judea to Samaria and to the ends of the earth (Matt. 28:19; Acts 1:8).

In other words, once the work of redemption had been achieved through the death and resurrection of Christ, the exclusiveness that had favored the Jews during Jesus' earthly ministry was lifted, and he could now draw everyone to himself into the new community (John 12:32). However, the historical process of God's progressive revelation required that, in chronological sequence, the gospel first be preached to the Jews and then to the Gentiles (Rom. 1:16).

The Jewish cultural environment within which Christ ministered with his first disciples was dominated by Judaism, the religion of the scribes and Pharisees that had developed after the Jews' return from the Babylonian exile. On many issues pertaining to belief and practice, Jesus was in violent disagreement with the teachings of Judaism. Yet, he had no choice but to work from within this environment to launch his worldwide ministry. He generally handled his differences with Judaism in one of three ways.

The first was direct confrontation about issues such as temple worship, tradition of the elders, legalism, Sabbath rules, etc. Those clashes became so threatening to the vested interests of the leaders of the people that they finally obtained Christ's sentencing as a rebel and his execution (Luke 19:47; 20:19; 22:2).

On other issues, Jesus was less adamant and more willing to make concessions. He sometimes backed away from clashing over matters of lesser importance to his program and went along with established traditions, but not without giving God's people the benefit of his own perspective (Matt. 8:4; 17:27; etc.).

Finally, Jesus chose the way of provisional accommodation for the sake of future implantation. He went along with undesirable situations in the sure knowledge that things would change after his resurrection. This strategy counted on the effect of delayed action—not to rock the boat for the present but prepare for the big change at the right time (Matt. 10:27; 12:14–16, 38–40; 13:24–30; 16:4; Mark 9:9–10; John 2:20–22; 4:21–23; etc.).

It is evident that the appointment of twelve male Jews as Jesus's first disciples falls into this third category. Since the first wave of the disciples' ministry was exclusively directed at Jews, it was inconceivable that anyone else but Jewish men could have been appointed to this task. Gentiles were generally held apart if not in contempt, and women were not deemed worthy of being instructed or of participating in Jewish public life, much less of being delegated as instructors to the people (Luke 7:6–7; John 4:9, 27; Acts 10:28). Therefore, under those conditions, it was inevitable that the first missionaries of the Christian movement should all be Jewish males. Had Jesus included Gentiles and women among the Twelve, he would have forfeited the future of the movement at its inception.

Theologically, the significance of Jesus' twelve apostles standing in judgment over the nation in lieu of the twelve patriarchs
would have been completely lost with the inclusion of women or
Gentiles among them (Matt. 19:28). On a more practical level,
the yet unregenerate hierarchical and competitive instincts of the
core disciples, who fought among themselves to be first and
greatest, would have stampeded any Gentile or woman among
them out of ministry (Mark 9:33–34; 10:35–37). Prejudice was
so ingrained that, several years after the launching of the church
at Pentecost, Jewish believers were surprised that Gentile believers could receive the Holy Spirit and become Christians without
first becoming Jews (Acts 10:45; 15:5).

Jesus' selection of the disciples bears witness to his patience
and flexibility. He was willing to accommodate temporarily with
the strictures that were imposed on him by the historical realities of the Jewish culture within which he ministered. But he also
knew that the day would come after his resurrection when the
floodgates would open wide for full inclusion in discipleship and,
therefore, in the ministry of the new community of all its members, regardless of race or gender (Matt. 28:19).

In the meantime, while Jesus acted with deference toward the
sensibilities of his cultural milieu so as not to jeopardize the future
of his mission, he was able to express his even greater commitment to the new community that he was dying (literally!) to create. So, if it was inexpedient for him to appoint women as part of
the Twelve, he did the next best thing. He encouraged a group
of women followers to travel with him and the Twelve and to minister alongside them on their itinerant mission (Luke 8:1–3).

As for the Gentiles, although Jesus could not integrate any of
them among his first disciples, he ministered to them both within
and outside of Jewish territory (Matt. 8:5–13; 15:21–28). After
his resurrection, he commanded his disciples to recruit other disciples among the Gentiles, thus making the call to discipleship
a universally accessible ministry (28:19; Acts 9:36). In this manner, he prepared for the full and unrestricted participation of all,
regardless of gender or racial origin, in the work of ministry.

This new openness for universally accessible ministry was emphatically recognized by the church on the very day of its inauguration at Pentecost (Acts 2:16–18). The great paradigm shift from old to new covenant did not occur at the beginning of Christ's earthly ministry but at its end (1 Cor. 11:25). History turned upon itself with the death and resurrection of Christ and with the subsequent coming of the Spirit at Pentecost. The first utterance made immediately after the outpouring of the Holy Spirit concerned a radical change in ministry roles. With the apostles at his side, Peter formally proclaimed that, because of the new era inaugurated by the coming of the Spirit, ministries that had been previously restricted were now universally accessible to all believers without distinctions of gender, age, or class. In obedience to the Great Commission, which Christ had entrusted to them a few days before, the disciples, represented by Peter, declared the empowerment of all believers to participate in the foremost ministry of the church as God's prophets and proclaimers of his gospel (Acts 2:16–18).

Consequently, anyone who claims today that women should not participate fully in the ministry of the church because Jesus's apostles were male simply does not understand the scriptural dynamic of the change that occurred from old covenant to new and instead tries to force on the church, Christ's new community, the standards of ancient Judaism. The argument that women should be barred from some church ministries because Christ's apostles were all men represents a regression to preresurrection conditions. Consistent adherence to this rule would require that not only women be excluded from ministry but also Gentiles, since Jesus and his apostles were Jews. Church leadership and ministry should then be only assumed by Jewish men.

To put it otherwise, to be consistent, Pope John-Paul II's contention that all priests should be male because Christ's apostles were male also requires that all priests be Jews because the apostles were Jews. Moreover, consistency also requires that priests be married, since the apostle Peter, the Pope's alleged predecessor, and other apostles were married (Matt. 8:14–15; 1 Cor.

9:5), and since only married men with families could become overseers (1 Tim. 3:2, 4). But thanks be to God that the New Testament declares all considerations of race, class, and gender irrelevant to the life of the church because of Christ's gift of oneness to the new community (Gal. 3:28).

5. *Spiritual Gifts*

In actual practice, the early church was generally able to live up to this ideal of total participation of its constituency in ministry. It soon discovered that God's provision for every believer's participation in the church's ministry was a divine enablement called "spiritual gifts." Sometimes, spiritual gifts are understood as something mystical that happens only to people who go through ecstatic spiritual experiences. However, the Scripture teaches that every believer who is part of a church body is, by that very fact, baptized of the Holy Spirit and "given the one Spirit to drink," which means that he or she receives to satiety the enablement necessary to function within that body (1 Cor. 12:13).

In this light, spiritual gifts may be defined as competencies, skills, and talents that are energized or generated by the Holy Spirit in order to be used for the common good (12:7), that is, for the edification and the building up of the church (14:4, 12). Scripture teaches that each believer has at least one such ability to contribute to the ministry of the church (12:11) and that no one may be excused or excluded from this responsibility (12:6, 15, 21).

In New Testament times, some church members were ignorant about spiritual gifts (12:1) while others were abusing them recklessly (14:23). Since many modern Christians are not doing much better in this regard, it should be the responsibility of every church to present a clear teaching about spiritual gifts so that its members have opportunity to discover, develop, and deploy their gifting and thus participate in the ministries of the church. There is such an abundance of literature and aids available today on this subject that every church can readily assist its members to define their spiritual gifts, and thus help them to participate in the priesthood of all believers by becoming servant-ministers in their communities.

Ignorance about spiritual gifts is a major reason for church dysfunction, but it is not the only one. Often sinful comparisons are allowed to create hierarchies of glamor, visibility, and status among ministries. Because some church ministries are more conspicuous than others, they can easily be surrounded with an aura of sacredness that elicits adulation of the person rather than humble gratitude for the gift. This is often the case with pulpit or altar ministries, whose practitioners can easily become the object of congregational devotion and admiration. By comparison, less visible and more menial tasks receive little attention or recognition. Consequently, some believers are reluctant to contribute their service because of its apparent insignificance (12:14–20).

Others demean the more humble forms of ministry and take pride in their own achievements (12:21–23). The Scripture emphatically counters such confusion with the principle that God gives the greater honor to ministries that are regarded as lowly, so that there might be no split-level stratification in the body, but all may be considered as equal (vv. 24–25). This principle of the equality of spiritual gifts is the practical expression of the oneness that binds the body together (v. 27). Should some ministries be considered "higher" or "greater" because of their constitutive importance to the body (v. 28), they do not confer any elitist advantage on their practitioners since anyone may eagerly desire the gifts that sustain such ministries (v. 31).

The New Testament definition of ministry requires nothing less than the full participation as co-servants of all the members of a congregation in carrying out the work of the church on the basis of each individual's spiritual gift(s). At the foot of the cross, the ground is level. In the church, no one is too lofty or too lowly to be exempt from doing ministry. To impose restrictions on such a divinely ordered plan or to allow defections from it can only result in churches that are dysfunctional in their ministry or disfigured as biblically authentic communities. The New Testament's vision for church ministry is nothing short of total mobilization of all the resources made available to it by the Holy Spirit.

Church leaders who, without justification, interfere with God's plan by excluding any of their members from full participation in gifts-based ministries take upon themselves a frightful responsibility. They prohibit Christians from fulfilling their God-assigned calling. Worse yet, they deprive the kingdom of the powerful potential invested in the church by its Lord for its growth and outreach.

Should it appear that a hermeneutical choice needs to be made between disobeying Scripture by opening ministry to all or disobeying Scripture by restricting ministry to some, it is obvious which form of disobedience would be less detrimental to the church. For those who believe there is a hermeneutical risk involved either way, the positive option should take precedence because of the debilitating effect upon God's work of the restrictive alternative. If error there is, it is better to stray helping the kingdom than cheating it.

A careful examination of scriptural data on the subject of ministry shows that, in New Testament times, both alternatives were practiced. Some churches had a policy of open ministry while others had to restrict ministry. Therefore, both models are biblically legitimate. As we will discover in the pages that follow, some churches qualify for the unrestricted priesthood of all believers while others must impose stringent limitations as to who may do ministry. One model will be called "normative" and the other "remedial."

6. The Normative Model for Church Ministry

The New Testament makes available two sources of information about the life and practice of early churches. One is the book of the Acts of the Apostles, which recounts the story of the beginning of churches in locations as diverse as Jerusalem, Rome, Corinth, and Ephesus. The other source is the New Testament letters, written to some of the same churches at a different time. Together, these documents provide insight into the circumstances, problems, and challenges that the first-century churches encountered in their development. Through their inspired authors, these writings provided the divine guidance needed by those churches. Those principles remain just as valid for the churches of our day.

a. Marching Orders From Jerusalem

The church was born on the day of Pentecost in Jerusalem. As mentioned above, the first declaration—direct, clear, indisputable—made on that day concerned the ministry of the church. Insofar as the Holy Spirit was now available to all, ministry was also open to all (Acts 2:17–18). The long-awaited outpouring of the Spirit at Pentecost signaled the beginning of the "last days," which will end with the "great and glorious day of the Lord" (v. 20), when the sun will go dark and the universe will collapse upon itself.

During the time bracketed between Pentecost and the End, three new developments are taking place because of the presence of the Holy Spirit. First, salvation becomes available to all who want it: "Everyone who calls on the name of the Lord will be saved" (v. 21). Second, what started at Pentecost will continue as God pours out his Spirit "on all people" (vv. 17–18). But the big news is that, because of this availability of the Holy Spirit to all believers, ministry is now accessible to all believers: "Sons and daughters will prophesy . . . servants, both men and women . . . will prophesy."

In both the Old and New Testaments, the ministry of prophecy is defined as the highest function for dispensing the Word of God (1 Cor. 12:28; 1 Peter 1:10–12; 2 Peter 1:20–21). The formal announcement by the apostle Peter on the day of Pentecost exploded former strictures and opened ministry to believers of all races ("all people") and of both genders ("men and women"). These marching orders for the church were never rescinded in Jerusalem. Their impact was felt even beyond

Jerusalem, from Judea to Caesarea, where both men and women were found prophesying (Acts 21:9–10). There can be no biblical oneness without shared ministry. In Jerusalem, "all the believers were one in heart and mind" (4:32). Such oneness could not have existed without equal access to ministry.

b. Oneness and Ministry Connection

The letter to the Romans was written to resolve a problem of racial prejudice within the congregation in Rome. The apostle Paul tried to convince Christian Jews and Christian Gentiles, who were in the same congregations but did not get along together, that since "God shows no partiality" (Rom. 2:11 RSV), they should accept one another just as Christ accepted them (15:7). In this context, Paul naturally emphasized the theme of oneness. His teaching here captured the essence of functional integration within the church: "Just as each of us has one body with many members, and these members do not all have the same function, so in Christ we who are many form one body, and each member belongs to all the others" (12:4–5).

Not surprisingly, as Paul described the diversity of ministries ("not all have the same function") within oneness ("we who are many form one body"), he discussed in the next sentence the diversity of gifts available in the body. His point was that each person who has a gift should use it optimally: "We have gifts that differ according to the grace given to us: prophecy, in proportion to faith; ministry, in ministering; the teacher, in teaching; the exhorter, in exhortation; the giver, in generosity; the leader, in diligence; the compassionate, in cheerfulness" (12:6–8 NRSV).

The strong statement about the link existing between oneness and gifts-based ministries that is made in this passage rules out all exclusions or exceptions. If any category of Christians had not been authorized to accede to some levels of ministry, this was Paul's perfect opportunity to mention it. Back in Jerusalem, when Peter made his great Pentecost declaration about universal access to ministry because of the outpouring of the Spirit, there were "visitors from Rome" in his audience, both Jews and Gentiles converted to Judaism (Acts 2:10–11). Inevitably, the church in Rome had eventually been informed of Peter's manifesto. Had Paul wanted to alter Peter's declared policy of open access to ministry and to replace it with a policy of exclusion, it would have been indispensable for him to do so in the context of this discussion on gifts and ministries. Such a change would have been big news that the Romans needed to know.

However, Paul makes no such teaching in Romans. To the contrary, believers are commanded to use their spiritual gifts to the maximum (Rom. 12:6–8). From all evidence, this was already happening. In the concluding greetings of this letter, Paul mentioned the names of many people, Jews and Gentiles, women and men, who were indiscriminately and happily engaged together in ministry, thus demonstrating authentic oneness (16:1–16).

In other words, the dominant teaching about ministry found in Romans is that people who have a spiritual gift should use it fully. It is inconceivable that, in a constitutional document of the church as influential as Paul's letter to the Romans has been through history, there should be found such strong encouragement for all to use their spiritual gifts to the fullest extent if any kind of curtailment on ministry had been part of the system of the New Testament church. Quite the opposite, the charge is for universal participation in ministry. The strong connection made in the New Testament between oneness and ministries leaves no room for exclusions.

A similar linkage between a discussion of the church as the community of oneness and an exhortation about spiritual gifts is found in 1 Corinthians 12. In this relatively large section, the apostle Paul insists that God activates spiritual gifts in everyone (v. 6), that "to each one the manifestation of the Spirit is given" (v. 7), and that gifts are "the work of one and the same Spirit, and he gives them to each one, just as he determines" (v. 11). Paul goes on to argue that body oneness can become a reality only as each believer uses his or her gift without hindrance (vv. 12–21).

This is the fullest and the most detailed discussion of oneness and spiritual gifts in the New Testament. The overriding emphasis is that spiritual gifts are to be used fully as an expression of the oneness of the body. No one has the right to claim exemption from participation for being different (vv. 14–16). Nor does the body consist of only one element or of one kind of members. Inclusive participation of the parts gives cohesion to the whole body (vv. 17–21). Paul's emphatic message is that there are no exemptions or limitations to full participation in the life and ministries of the body. If there were any exceptions to this rule, they did not apply to the Corinthian church. In fact, the Corinthian Christians were forbidden by Paul to make exceptions (vv. 15, 21).

This letter contains two indications, one positive and the other negative, of how this principle of total participation in ministry was played out in practice. The positive reference cites a man and a woman praying and prophesying (1 Cor. 11:4–5). The ministry functions were identical for the man and the woman, except for one difference, which had to do with attire. When the man led in worship or spoke God's word, he had to keep his head uncovered. But when the woman led in worship or spoke God's word, she had to wear a head covering. In the same passage, Paul stated that a woman's hair is given to her as a covering (v. 15), thus making the head covering redundant and reducing the roles difference between men and women in ministry to practically nothing.

The seemingly negative indication is cited in 1 Corinthians 14:33b–36. At first sight, this statement startles. It reads like a flagrant contradiction of what Paul taught on ministry in the rest of this letter. It enjoins absolute silence for women in church— not a sound, not even a whisper to ask a question. Far from praying and prophesying (11:5), women may not even be learners in church. If they have questions, they must wait to be home, where their husbands will answer them. If they don't have husbands, they presumably don't get answers. The reasons adduced for this prohibition are even more astounding: the practice of other churches (v. 33), legal requirements (v. 34), and standards of church propriety (v. 35).

Because this statement violates everything Paul had written elsewhere on oneness and gifts-based ministries within the church, most commentators interpret this passage not to refer to ministry but to conduct. They theorize that women were interfering with church services by talking loudly among themselves and by interrupting worship to ask inopportune questions. According to this scenario, Paul was telling them to keep quiet and not disturb proceedings. Women could participate in the ministry of the church provided they behaved properly; but when they didn't behave, they had to sit it out.

As ingenious as it seems, this interpretation does not do justice to the difficulties that distinguish the text under consideration as an exegetical minefield. The point of this section is that women may not minister. Men only can perform ministry while women sit under them in total and submissive silence. The rationales offered in the text to justify the prohibition are intended to make it permanently binding for all women. Because it is presented as the practice of "all the congregations of the saints," substantiated by what "the Law says" and confirmed by church protocol, the prohibition is intended to have absolute and universal application.

However, the appeals to alleged and otherwise unconfirmed church practice and protocols in order to silence women brutally violate everything Paul wrote in this very letter about the inclusion in ministry of every member of the body. Moreover, the appeal to the Law sounds hollow, since there is no item of legislation in the Old Testament that forbids women to speak and requires them to be in submission. Moreover, it would be contrary to Paul's view of the old covenant to invoke the law as the definer of Christian worship (2 Cor. 3:5–6, 14–18; Gal. 3:10, 23–26; etc.).

Had this teaching come from Paul, he would not have based it on justifications as flimsy as church practice that changes with time, a law that isn't there but which was probably imported from the synagogue, and ecclesiastical conventions about what may or may not be shameful. The apostle did have at his disposal a decisive scriptural argument to validate this kind of prohibition. This irrefutable argument came out of the temptation story (Gen. 3:1–6), which he used elsewhere in support of a similar prohibition (1 Tim. 2:13–14).

In this other church, women were to "learn in quietness and full submission" (1 Tim. 2:11). They could not teach or have authority over men from fear that they would fall into error as Eve did when she was deceived and became a transgressor. There is evidence in the Corinthian correspondence that Paul was aware of this argument at the time of writing since he used it in the form of a warning to the church in Corinth (2 Cor. 11:3). It is unlikely that Paul would set aside this powerful argument to base his appeal on the shaky and easily refutable considerations as outlined above. Such statements do not reflect the rigor and the sharpness of his thought.

The most likely explanation for the contradictions created by the prohibition may well be that here, as in several other places in 1 Corinthians, Paul was quoting disapprovingly the teachings propounded in Corinth by opponents who were trying to sabotage his work (see my book, *Beyond Sex Roles*, Baker, 1985, pp. 144–53, 283–88). There is evidence that some Judaic-oriented teachers followed Paul, trying to wreck the churches he established by claiming they were not Jewish enough (Gal. 1:7; 4:17; 5:10, 12). The same people who came from "the congregations of the saints" (1 Cor. 14:33b), an early designation for churches within Judaism, surely objected to Paul's policy of open access to ministry of all believers. By intimidating female believers with contrived arguments, they could reduce by half the ministry potential of the Corinthian church and protect their own vested interests as male leaders.

The immediate context of the Judaizers' prohibition supports this interpretation. Just above it, Paul had reiterated the principle of universal access to ministry when he stated, "You can all prophesy" (1 Cor. 14:31). Then he mentioned the need for order and peace during worship (vv. 32–33a). This gave him the opportunity to tackle the contention caused in Corinth by false teachers, who were disrupting the congregation by trying to impede women's ministries. So, he quoted their teaching to show how outrageous it was compared to his own teaching about gifts-based ministries (vv. 33b–35). He then scathingly exclaimed in verse 36, as it were, "What kind of teaching is this? Is this something new that God has given you or are you the only ones God favors with this teaching?" Paul then went on to make it clear to all in Corinth, and especially to one of his leading opponents who claimed to be "a prophet or spiritually gifted" (v. 37a), that his own teaching was not based on church traditions or on the law, as was the Judaizers' teaching, but that it was based on "the Lord's command" (v. 37b). And should this troublemaker refuse to come to reason, then the Corinthians should just ignore him (v. 38).

Unfortunately, quotation marks had not been invented when Paul wrote his letters. Quotes had to be recognized by the content and context of the citation. Had they been available to him, Paul would surely have set the prohibition statement (vv. 33b–35) between quotation marks as a teaching he rejected. For this reason, this text is reported here as a negative indication, giving a positive insight on the practice of gifts-based ministries in Corinth. As in Jerusalem and in Rome, the oneness of the body was expressed in Corinth by unhindered and total participation of the members of the body in the ministry of the body.

The connection that has been consistently traced between authentic community and full participation in ministry on the basis of spiritual gifts is also found in other letters. In Ephesians, Paul exhorted his readers to live a life worthy of the calling they had received (Eph. 4:1). This calling was to develop relationships of humility, love, and peace, which would preserve the unity of the Spirit (vv. 2–3). Because the Spirit is at work, he creates one body (v. 4). This body is neither multiple nor fragmented. It is not subdivided into a ruling part and a subject part. Since only Christ is the head of this body, it may not legitimately have additional heads (5:23). Humans who masquerade as earthly heads of the church are usurping the headship of Christ and disfigure his church. Just as the creator of the church is "one Spirit," "one Lord," "one Father," so the body made by him can only be "one" (4:4–6).

This oneness is made possible through the gifts graciously provided to the church by the ascended Christ (vv. 7–8). Many of these gifts pertain to the word of God, which is preached and taught for the purpose of equipping the whole body to do the work of ministry (vv. 11–12). As a result, the body is built up into oneness, into the image of Christ (vv. 12–13).

The letter to the Ephesians was devoted mainly to the definition of the church as the community of oneness. With other New Testament documents, it established a strong link between oneness and ministry while describing both as the result of the total involvement of all the members of the body, without any mention of exclusions or exemptions.

A similar pattern is found in 1 Peter—and well it should, since Peter was the one who proclaimed open access to ministry for all believers on Pentecost (Acts 2:16–18). After affirming the ultimacy of love as the relational mode among Christians ("above all," 1 Peter 4:8), the apostle exhorts all believers to use the spiritual gifts they have received. By so doing, they will not only serve God but will also become servants of each other (vv. 10–11). The full participation of each one is commanded in this letter, again without reference to any exclusionary provision.

In summary, a consistent pattern may thus be traced from the book of Acts through the letters of the New Testament. The church is described as a community of love and oneness. A normal expression of this oneness is unrestricted involvement of all believers in the ministry of the community. Since this ministry is carried out with each individual contributing his or her spiritual gift, the expectation is for all to use their gifts to the fullest. Instructions that would impede or curtail anyone's participation in church ministry on the basis of race, class, or gender are present neither in the letters surveyed above nor in any other document of the New Testament, with the exception discussed below. Evidently, God is an equal opportunity employer.

Through the cumulative force of the argument from silence, a strong case can be made that, since no exception is mentioned in those documents about selective access to church ministries, such ministries are open to all qualified believers without restrictions. But such an approach is not necessary since the consistent pattern in those documents is not one of silence but of emphatic affirmation: To honor God, all must be fully involved in the ministries that correspond to their gifting. For this reason, it is appropriate to designate this pattern of church ministry, as generally advocated in the New Testament, "normative."

7. The Remedial Model of Church Ministry

The Pastoral Letters, a name referring collectively to Paul's two letters to Timothy and his letter to Titus, present an entirely different picture of church ministry. This fact does not mean that it is unbiblical or less important. It is a legitimate biblical model that must be followed as needed. The analysis that follows will help define the conditions that call for the application of this model.

When Paul wrote his first letter to Timothy, the latter was the apostle's envoy extraordinaire in Ephesus, a troubleshooting missionary delegated to the Ephesian church to put out the fires of heresy that had been lit by false teachers (1 Tim. 1:3–4). Titus had been sent to Crete, a Mediterranean island south of the Greek peninsula, to accomplish a similar mission (Titus 1:5, 10–14). Both letters contain abundant data relative to the practice of ministry in Ephesus and Crete at the time when the apostle Paul wrote them, close to the end of his life. This information can easily be compared to what is known of the practice of other New Testament churches.

The evidence shows the existence of an inverse relation between open congregational participation in ministry on one hand, and heavy leadership structures that monopolized ministry on the other. Whenever allowance was made for congregational participation in ministry, the leadership structure receded into the background. However, whenever ministry opportunities were denied to the congregation or to segments of it, ministry was assumed by the leadership.

a. Exceptional Prominence

Compared to what is known of the practice of ministry in other New Testament churches, both 1 Timothy and Titus present a leadership structure that is considerably more prominent.

In the Jerusalem church, the apostles were the original leaders. Soon, others were added to their numbers. A group later called the Seven was chosen by the congregation (Acts 6:3, 5; cf. 21:8). Two of them carried out ministries identical to that of the apostles (6:8–10; 8:5–8, 40; 21:8). They were joined by elders (15:6), who eventually assumed leadership by themselves and with James, the half-brother of Jesus (21:17–18). This trajectory shows a flexible structure of leadership that adapted to changing circumstances and need, and which was shared with the whole congregation in significant instances of corporate decision-making (6:3, 5; 15:22–23).

The church in Rome became an important center of Christian activity and influence during Paul's lifetime, to the extent that the faith of the Roman Christians was "being reported all over the world" (Rom. 1:8). In the course of his letter to them, Paul made mention of "different gifts," some of them implying leadership functions (12:6–8). However, any acknowledgment of personalized leadership ministries is absent. Although the apostle greeted by name over two dozen friends, relatives, and co-workers who were in Rome at the time of writing, the letter contains no reference to overseers, elders, bishops, or deacons (16:3–15). The only exceptions were a man and a woman whom he called "apostles," probably in the broad sense of the term (v. 7), and Phoebe, a *diakonos* ("deacon") from another church, delegated by Paul to Rome with a mission. (vv. 1–2).

It is inconceivable that a leadership structure was not present in the Roman church. This church was afflicted with serious relational problems that threatened its unity and would have justified the strong intervention of its leaders (2:1–5, 17–24; 14:10–

13). But Paul did not submit these matters to their jurisdiction. For whatever reason, he bypassed them completely as he instructed and admonished the congregation directly through the letter. It was as if leaders did not exist. They did not even rate a greeting as titular office-holders or an acknowledgment of their service in Rome. Leaders and leadership issues were apparently not of paramount importance for Paul or for the church in Rome when he wrote this letter. He was much more interested in the body ministering to itself at grassroots level (12:9–10, 16–18; 13:8–10; 14:1–4; 15:1–7), since he was convinced that his readers were "competent to instruct one another" (15:14).

Although "elders" were appointed in the churches planted by Paul during his missionary journeys (Acts 14:23), they are neither mentioned nor greeted in any of his letters save the Pastorals. This omission becomes most glaring in his correspondence with the church in Corinth. Paul had originally labored for more than a year and a half in that city. Subsequently, he made two return visits to it. This relationship gave him ample opportunity to establish a leadership structure within that church. There was a superabundance of spiritual gifts in Corinth, so that prophets and teachers were presumably present in the congregation (1 Cor. 12:28).

However, there is no evidence relative to the presence of a functioning leadership structure in the Corinthian church. The church was rife with problems such as divisions, personality conflicts, immorality, lawsuits, sacrilegious worship, lifestyle issues, doctrinal challenges, and false teachers who claimed to be apostles. Each of those situations would have provided enough reason for the forceful intervention of local church leaders. But according to 1 and 2 Corinthians, elders, overseers, and deacons were not part of Paul's strategy to reform the Corinthian church. There is no reference in these letters to such functions. Paul chose to address, rebuke, exhort, and command the congregation directly. Hortatory challenges abound in the letters ("I command you," "I want you to know," "I appeal to you," etc.) When an important action was to be taken, the whole congregation "assembled in the name of [the] Lord Jesus Christ" was commanded to do so (1 Cor. 5:4).

There were capable people in the Corinthian congregation, worthy of exercising leadership. "The household of Stephanas were the first converts" in that region. This couple of veteran Christians had proven their loyalty by devoting "themselves to the service of the saints." Therefore, the apostle urged the Corinthians "to submit to such as these and to everyone who joins in the work and labors at it" (16:15–16). Instead of calling on a leadership organization to take matters in hand and to govern one of his most turbulent congregations, Paul preferred to "urge" the faithful to submit to the guidance of one servant family from among them and of other undesignated workers whose validation was their goodwill and service. The inevitable presence of at least one female in the household of Stephanas and the open-ended inclusivity of "everyone who joins in the work" contrast sharply with the stringent specifications for positions of leadership found in the Pastorals. Paul's closing entreaty reveals his heart in the matter. He preferred the congregation to be able to fix its own problems as a self-reliant body: "Put things in order, listen to my appeal, agree with one another, live in peace" (2 Cor. 13:11 NRSV).

The churches Paul had established in Galatia came under the impact of a false teaching that was intended to take them back into the bondage of Judaic law. This was a classic case for strong local leadership to rise and take control of the situation. Yet, in Paul's letter to the Galatians, the only positive reference to local leadership function is a notation concerning the remuneration of teachers, which actually validated their teaching ministry among the Galatians (Gal. 6:6). Paul invoked castration on the false teachers (5:12), but he made sure the faithful ones were getting paid. Evidently there was leadership in the Galatian churches that remained loyal to Paul and his gospel. But the apostle did not involve them pointedly in the Galatians' struggle against heresy.

In other words, establishing a new leadership network or improving a faulty one was not Paul's solution to the Galatian crisis. He assumed that the Galatian congregations could take care of themselves, and he addressed his appeal to them broadly, asking them to reject false teachings and to conform to the views that he had taught them (5:7–10). Despite the relatively serious crisis in the Galatian churches, overseers, elders, or deacons were not called upon to intervene, according to this letter.

The letter to the Ephesians is almost entirely devoted to the doctrine of the church, describing the ultimacy of the church in God's purposes. It defines the nature of the church as the community of oneness and prescribes the conduct and relationships that befit life in community. If an elaborate leadership system had been deemed essential to the proper functioning of every church, this was the perfect occasion to include the description of an ideal governance structure that would have been valid for all churches, at all times and in all places.

Unlike most other New Testament letters, Ephesians is not an action letter. It was not written to respond to a crisis or to a specific need. It simply tells what the church is about. As such, the letter does not address any circumstance at the time of writing that necessitated the intervention of a team of leaders. It contains no specific reference to overseers, elders, or deacons. This is all the more remarkable since the same letter carefully lays out a domestic code to delineate the organization of Christian households (Eph. 5:21–6:9). But there are no parallel instructions for the organization of the church apart from the command for all believers to "submit to one another out of reverence for Christ" (5:21).

In his discussion of spiritual gifts, the apostle indeed listed some ministries graciously provided by the ascended Christ to the church at large (4:11). But this list was generic, not personalized to the local situation in Ephesus. Despite the absence of any mention in Ephesians of any specific overseers, elders, and deacons, it is unlikely that the local church was devoid of leaders. But their invisibility in this letter suggests that the life and the organization of the church were not designed to revolve around a leadership structure. Rather, the leadership structure was ancillary to the life of the community and entered into action only when and as needed.

The letter to the Philippians is the only Pauline letter apart from the Pastorals that contains any reference to bishops (or overseers) and deacons (Phil. 1:1). Finally, we find overseers and deacons! However, in this case, they do not seem to be very active. They are politely acknowledged in the opening salutation of the letter, but then they completely disappear.

At the time of writing, things were relatively quiet in the church at Philippi. But there was an actual crisis in the form of a major personality conflict. Two women leaders who had served as co-workers with Paul and other men were at each other's throats. Their dispute no doubt had a negative effect on the assembly. This would be a textbook case for intervention by the leadership of the church—unless the two women were themselves the leadership group, which is entirely possible in view of the origins of the Philippian church (Acts 16:13–15). Surprisingly, Paul did not ask the overseers and/or deacons to help the women get together and reconcile. Instead, he pleaded with them "to agree with each other in the Lord." Then, he called on one individual with no other title but "loyal yokefellow" to "help these women" (Phil. 4:2–3). Whenever possible, the apostle seemed to prefer to call on the body to minister to itself rather than to invoke top-down authoritarian resolution methods.

The letter to the Colossians has in common with Romans that Paul was writing to a church he had never visited. It would seem that one of his concerns for those churches would have been the implementation of leadership systems that would conform to his standards. Therefore, one might expect those two letters to contain some instructions about the call to become overseer, elder, or deacon, about their character qualifications, marital status, and management of their household, and about their lifestyle, the length of their Christian experience, and their reputation with outsiders.

Not only are such instructions absent in those letters, but any mention of leaders to whom such instructions could have been relevant is simply not there. Instead, Paul exhorted the laypeople in both congregations to assume responsibility toward each other since they were "competent to instruct one another" (Rom. 15:14) and "to teach and admonish one another" because the word of Christ dwelt in them richly (Col. 3:16). It appears that, under normal circumstances, the apostle Paul was more interested in encouraging believers to minister to each other than in setting up orders of hierarchy for their governance.

This enumeration could go on with every New Testament letter, only to confirm this finding. Whatever leadership structures existed in the early churches, they were inconspicuous, discreet, self-effacing, and flexible. They seem to have adapted their activities and visibility to local circumstances and needs. Clearly evident is a concern not to preempt congregational initiative and involvement. The leadership of New Testament churches seems to stand on the sidelines, ready to intervene only in situations of necessity. They are invisible servants, whose role is to equip the body.

By and large, in the New Testament, leaders are not enjoined or permitted to exercise authority over their flocks. True, the people under their care are instructed to obey them and submit to them, as well they should, but the leaders are themselves under accountability (Heb. 13:17). Their style of leadership must therefore derive from eagerness to serve so that they do not lord it over their flock but lead them by being examples (1 Peter 5:1–4). Apparently, leadership structures and authority issues were not of primary concern in most New Testament churches. Total participation of the entire church in ministry, which would translate into energy, growth, and outreach, held priority.

Turning to the Pastoral Letters, however, is like being transported into a different world. Suddenly, the presence of overseers, elders, and deacons becomes massive and unavoidably manifest (1 Tim. 3:1–13; 5:17–22; Titus 1:5–9). Leaders suddenly march out of the shadows and stand at center stage.

No other document or group of documents in the New Testament contains as much information and as many instructions about overseers, elders, and deacons as found in 1 Timothy and Titus. Those two letters alone have sixteen verses that deal with overseers and elders, in contrast to only three references in all other New Testament letters, for a total of only seven verses (Phil. 1:1; James 5:14; 1 Peter 5:1–5). Viewed differently, in 110 chapters of New Testament letters, only seven verses pertain to overseers and elders, in contrast to sixteen verses in the nine chapters of 1 Timothy and Titus.

In the non-Pastoral letters, leaders are invisible servants who work on the sidelines to equip and support the congregations. In the Pastorals, people become leaders because they "desire a noble task" (1 Tim. 3:1), for which they must command "proper respect" (3:4) and have "a good reputation" (3:7). Consequently, they obtain "an excellent standing" (3:13), and some become "worthy of double honor" (5:17). Leaders are no shrinking violets in these letters. Instead, they stand out from among the ranks. Not only are they prominent but they are also preeminent.

The exceptional prominence given to overseers, elders, and deacons in the Pastoral Letters requires an explanation. It would be simplistic to theorize that this importance in the Pastorals is due to the fact that church organization was the subject matter of these letters. This is no explanation; it is simply a statement of fact. The real issue is: Why was church organization the subject matter of these two letters when it received such scant attention in the other letters?

Other congregations had been founded prior to the churches in Ephesus and Crete, some of which were also beset with serious problems. Similar to the churches in Ephesus and Crete, the situation of churches in Galatia and Corinth called for the intervention of strong leadership. Yet, all the evidence found in Acts and Paul's letters relative to those churches indicates that the apostle expected them to resolve their problems without the intervention of such leadership structures as are described in the Pastorals. Such a system of church organization was an innovation in early church history. Had it been standard practice, there would have been no need to describe it in detail in the Pastorals and to advocate its urgent implementation.

The issue of the timing of Paul's instructions about church order as reflected in the Pastorals is even more baffling. Prior to writing 1 Timothy, Paul had been interacting with the Ephesians over a period of some fifteen years. This included a time of ministry in Ephesus at the end of his second missionary journey, a three-year stay during the third missionary journey, a separate meeting with the Ephesian elders, and the writing of the letter to the Ephesians. There was no other church where Paul had spent as much time as in Ephesus. Should he have wanted to implant a leadership-intensive form of government in Ephesus, Paul had many opportunities to do so prior to his writing 1 Timothy. He could have done so even more effectively when he was on location in Ephesus. The singularity of the leadership structure he prescribed for Ephesus in 1 Timothy after all this time must be explained.

b. Exceptional Dominance

Compared to what is known of the practice of ministry in other New Testament churches, both 1 Timothy and Titus present a leadership structure that is dominant.

In a few decades, the early church movement spread like wildfire through the ancient world. One of the secrets for this rapid expansion was total lay involvement in the ministries of the local churches. In whatever city or town targeted by the apostle Paul and other missionaries, Christian communities sprouted with a life of their own. From Jerusalem to Rome, in the shadow of pagan temples and on the edges of the Forum, there were little groups of believers animated with a passionate commitment to each other and to their corporate mission. The book of Acts and most of the New Testament letters are permeated with the euphoria and the vitality of churches where everyone was involved in body life and ministry. Under normal circumstances, therefore, the apostle Paul was more interested in encouraging Christian folks to minister to each other and together than in setting up orders of hierarchy for their governance.

This sense of infectious effervescence is lacking in the Pastoral Letters. The crisis that had impacted the congregations of Ephesus and Crete had left them in a state of disarray and dependency. A measure of the downfall of the Ephesians is indicated by their need to receive instructions so that they would "know how people ought to conduct themselves in God's household" (1 Tim. 3:15). After heroic beginnings, multiple victories, and fifteen years of existence, the church had regressed into infancy. They had to relearn everything from the beginning.

Had the church stayed on course, Paul's first letter to Timothy might have contained warm commendations for the believers' progress in the ways of Christ, for their devotion to his kingdom, for the increase of their mutual love and spirit of reciprocal self-sacrifice, for their commitment to develop their spiritual gifts and to expand their ministries, and for the success of their outreach beyond the churches they had previously planted during the days when he could pray for them with thanksgiving (Eph. 1:15–16). Instead, he had to write them a hard letter with warnings, stern advice, urgings, and commands.

Ephesians and 1 Timothy were written to the same congregation a few years apart. Yet content-wise, they are worlds apart. Even a cursory comparison of the rich theological content of Ephesians with the basic instructional precepts of 1 Timothy shows how far the Ephesian church had strayed from its first love (cf. also Rev. 2:4). First Timothy contains no references to oneness, to spiritual gifts, to shared ministries, or to the life of the Spirit. The Holy Spirit is mentioned only incidentally and never in relation to his ministry within the believer or to the community (1 Tim. 3:16; 4:1). The church itself is not described as a live and dynamic body but in static and institutional terms, such as the "pillar and foundation of the truth" (3:15).

According to the Pastorals, professional leaders are definitely the ones in charge of church ministry. They do ministry while the congregations remain mostly passive. It is the leaders who are "entrusted with God's work" (Titus 1:7). Meanwhile, the other members of the congregation pray so that they can live peaceful and quiet lives (1 Tim. 2:2). The men pray with hands uplifted while the widows pray night and day, asking God for help (2:8; 5:5). Women do "good deeds" (2:10); widows do "good deeds" (5:10); the rich do "good deeds" (6:18); everybody does "good deeds" (Titus 3:8, 14). There are more references to "good deeds" in the Pastorals than in all the other books of the New Testament put together. Good deeds seem to have become a substitute for spiritual gifts-based ministries.

The ministries that derive from spiritual gifts and normally devolve on the congregation were being performed in Ephesus and Crete, but not by the congregation. They were entrusted to professional leaders. The overseers/elders were the ones responsible to preach and teach, to "encourage others by sound doctrine," and to "refute" those who opposed it (1 Tim. 3:2; 4:11– 16; 5:17; Titus 1:9; 2:1). The same leaders also doubled up as those who managed the life of the church, who took "care of God's church," and who "[directed] the affairs of the church" (1 Tim. 3:5; 5:17). Obviously, this monopoly on ministry did not leave the rest of the people much to do except those "good deeds" that were already incumbent on every Christian.

Teaching and preaching became strictly monitored ministries in Ephesus. Timothy was to teach and preach until the time of Paul's projected visit there (1 Tim. 4:11, 13). But in so doing, he was to watch his doctrine closely (4:16) or pay close attention to his own teaching (NRSV). The overseers/elders were selected in function of their ability to teach (3:2); the deacons had no teaching attributions (vv. 8–13). In this letter, the apostle instituted a system of remuneration for elders whose work was preaching and teaching (5:17). To give exceptional recognition to those ministries, he required that their practitioners receive double salary. He justified this exclusive largesse by citing Scripture from the Old Testament and from Jesus' own teaching (v. 18; cf. Deut. 25:4; Luke 10:7). He thus made teaching and preaching at this stage in the life of the Ephesian church appointive functions with high visibility by virtue of this remuneration.

In the light of Paul's insistence on the need to protect "sound doctrine," it becomes clear that such policies were intended to entrust the responsibility of teaching and preaching to carefully selected individuals. The critical church situation that had developed in Ephesus required that "reliable men" or "faithful people" (NRSV) specially trained for this purpose by Timothy be the ones "qualified to teach others" (2 Tim. 2:2; cf. 1 Tim. 3:2, 5:17; Titus 1:9). By necessity, all the other church members, both men and women, were on the receiving end of the teaching. This concern was similar to that expressed in the letter of James, to the effect that "not many of you should presume to be teachers" (James 3:1). Even when they have the spiritual gift of teaching, untrained or previously disqualified persons must be willing to learn quietly before aspiring to teach (1 Tim. 2:11; 2 Tim. 2:2).

The standard for managing the church properly was set by how the overseer took care of his own family, especially by making sure that his children obeyed him "with proper respect" (1 Tim. 3:4). When leaders failed to "direct the affairs of the church well," they only got half pay (though, apparently, they could not get fired for incompetence; 5:17). Only misbehavior that could be attested by two or three witnesses could draw "public rebuke" (5:19–20). Undoubtedly, the high degree of immunity accorded to the overseers/elders provided the congregations with a relatively stable leadership structure. But what the church may have gained in stability through such policies, it may have lost in leadership accountability and, therefore, in quality of ministry.

The attributions of the overseers/elders suggest that they had a virtual monopoly on ministry. They fulfilled the ministries of the Word, like preaching and teaching, as well as the ministries of community care and management. It is difficult to conceive that much could have been left for anyone else to do. Moreover, in the Ephesian church Paul also gave instructions for another group of officers, the deacons. Although their job description is not spelled out, they apparently had important functions since the qualification requirements for the diaconate were almost as stringent as those for the overseer/elder position (3:8–13).

Finally, in both Ephesus and Crete, there was another level of leadership endowed with a high degree of authority. Timothy and Titus had been delegated by Paul to these wayward churches as pro tem reformers to salvage what was left of them. As such, they were invested with exceptional powers. Timothy could command (1:3; 4:11), teach (4:11, 13; 6:2), preach (4:13), give instructions to the people (5:7), and lay hands to designate other leaders (5:22). Likewise, Titus was supposed to appoint elders (1:5), teach (2:1–2, 7, 9, 15), and "encourage and rebuke with all authority" (2:15). Such offices were exceptional and temporary but power intensive. Except for the apostle himself, no other single worker in any of the local churches referred to in the New Testament is described as having had as much authority and visibility as Timothy in Ephesus and Titus in Crete.

As necessary as it may have been in those churches, the shift from congregation-based ministries to functionary type, staff-driven ministries did not occur without loss. The radicalness, intensity, and audacity that characterized other New Testament churches are simply not reflected in the Pastorals. These churches seem to have become paralyzed under the impact of some trauma that impaired them and required the refereed appointment of an elaborate, multi-layered, top-heavy structure of leadership in order to make them operative again. The situation of clergy dominance requires an explanation.

c. Exceptional Exclusions

Compared to what is known of ministry practices in other New Testament churches, both 1 Timothy and Titus present a leadership structure that is extremely restrictive.

According to Acts and most of the New Testament letters, the procedure for appointing church members to their respective ministries was simple (Acts 6:3; Rom. 12:4–8; 1 Cor. 12:4–11). Every member of the body who was in good standing within the community had to discover his or her spiritual gift and assume a ministry that matched the gift. The integration of the various ministries within the body was a corporate function of the body (1 Cor. 12:20–25).

The appointment of the Seven provides a case in point (Acts 6:3). Seven men were needed to perform a specific task in the Jerusalem church. Their selection was made on the basis of three criteria. First, they were affirmed by the community. By virtue of their selection, the community vouched for their character and reputation ("select among yourselves seven men of good standing," NRSV). Second, they were "known to be full of the Spirit," which meant that they cultivated their spiritual walk and used their spiritual gifts. Third, they had to be full of "wisdom," which meant that they were people of experience and discernment.

Except for the Pastoral Letters, there is no reference in the New Testament to additional specifications needed to qualify for ministry, including ministries of leadership. In particular, the marital status of candidates is never brought up as a determinant consideration. One of the Seven, Philip, had four daughters and, therefore, was or had been married. The daughters themselves were prophets but unmarried (Acts 21:9). The apostle Paul was unmarried (1 Cor. 7:8; 9:5), and he urged people who wanted to devote themselves in full freedom to "the Lord's affairs" to remain single (7:32–35). In this, Paul echoed Christ's teaching about the acceptance of singleness as a special calling (cf. 7:7), voluntarily assumed for greater usefulness in the kingdom ("others have renounced marriage because of the kingdom of heaven," Matt. 19:12).

The contrast with the Pastorals is brutal! Suddenly, in 1 Timothy and Titus, the ministries of the Word and of oversight and management, as well as those pertaining to other tasks like the deacon functions, required that they be entrusted to married men: A bishop (or "overseer") must be "the husband of but one wife" (1 Tim. 3:2); "a deacon must be the husband of but one wife" (v. 12); an elder must be "the husband of but one wife" (Titus 1:6). Moreover, such a man had to have children in order to hold office: An overseer has his own family and children (1 Tim. 3:4); a deacon must have children and a household (v. 12); an elder must be one who has children (Titus 1:6). And finally, those children must be obedient: An overseer must "see that his children obey him with proper respect" (1 Tim. 3:4); a deacon "must manage his children and his household well" (v. 12); only a man whose children are believers and "not open to the charge of being wild and disobedient" may become an elder (Titus 1:6).

Nowhere else in the New Testament are there such requirements in order to qualify for ministry. To the contrary, both Jesus and Paul clearly indicate a preference for Christian workers to remain single for the sake of ministry. Over against this, the Pastorals categorically and repeatedly exclude from key ministries anyone but married men with obedient children.

In other words, according to the Pastoral Letters, the following categories of believers do not qualify for those ministries regardless of their worthiness and the legitimacy of their spiritual gifts: single men, married men with no children, married men with only one child, married men with at least one child who is disobedient, and women—who are out altogether (1 Tim. 2:12).

This drastically reductive model of access to ministry is the opposite of the New Testament pattern of spiritual gifts-based ministries. However, it is in the Scriptures and thus may not be dismissed. But the massive contradictions it creates for the definition of ministry compared to the teaching of the rest of the New Testament requires explanation.

d. The Explanation

This explanation may be found along two lines of inquiry. The first is the history of the churches in Ephesus and Crete; the other, the contents of the Pastoral Letters themselves.

(1) The history of Paul's dealings with the church in Ephesus shows that it was his toughest assignment. Ephesus represented one of Paul's largest, most demanding, most difficult, and most

dangerous church planting endeavors. According to Acts, it was the only church where his service was continuously accompanied with tears (Acts 20:19, 31). It was the only place where his ministry met with the opposition of both Jews and Gentiles (19:8–9, 23–31). Ephesus was the only place where he had to contend successively with sectarians (vv. 1–7), with the synagogue (vv. 8–9), with occult practices (vv. 13–20), and with temple idolatry (vv. 23–41). At the same time, Paul never stopped discipling the faithful night and day for a period of three years and evangelizing among Jews and Greeks (20:18–21, 31).

His efforts did not go unrewarded. All the Greeks and the Jews who lived in Ephesus and in the surrounding province of Asia heard the word of the Lord through Paul's ministry (19:10, 26). But such results were achieved at great personal cost. It was during this time that Paul "fought with wild beasts in Ephesus" (1 Cor. 15:32) and that he came "under great pressure," far beyond his ability to endure so that "he despaired even of life" because he "felt the sentence of death" in his heart (2 Cor. 1:8–9). The Ephesian church was planted in circumstances of extreme hardship with blood, sweat, and tears.

The apostle's burden for Ephesus did not lift with his departure from that city. On the way back from his third missionary journey, he sent for the elders of the Ephesian church for an unprecedented emergency meeting (Acts 20:17–38). During this gathering, he proceeded to defend the integrity of his ministry, which, apparently, had come under attack at Ephesus (vv. 18–21, 33–35). Even more importantly, Paul gave an anguished warning to the Ephesian elders about a disaster that would soon befall their congregation. He predicted that their church would come under attack from two sides. The first onslaught would be external, as "savage wolves" would come among the flock to destroy it. The other source of trouble would be internal; homegrown heretics would rise from among themselves and split the congregation.

In the face of this depressing prospect, all Paul could do was to urge the elders to remain alert (vv. 28, 31–32). Not only was the Ephesian church the one ministry that caused him the most pain, but it was also the only one about which he predicted that the flock would be devastated under the impact of false teachers, some of whom were hiding among the elders who embraced him for the last time at dockside near Miletus (v. 30).

Although Paul's letter to the Ephesians may have been a circular letter intended for a broader readership than just the congregation in Ephesus, it reflects some of his concerns. On a theoretical level, the apostle wanted the Ephesians to understand the nature and the workings of the church as community (Eph. 2–5). On the practical side, he tried to consolidate the spiritual commitment of the Ephesians to help them face the predicted storm. He assured them of his prayers so that they would know God better and would be enlightened about the nobility of their calling (1:17–18). He urged them to divest themselves of their old selves and to be renewed in their minds in order to "not give the devil a foothold" (4:22–27). In anticipation of "the devil's schemes," he offered them a protective armor to help them survive the cosmic battle that would soon engulf them as they became the target of the coordinated attacks of rulers and authorities, of the powers of this dark world, and of the spiritual forces of evil in the heavenly realms (6:11–18).

From all evidence, when Paul wrote his first letter to Timothy, the predicted onslaught had been unleashed; the storm had hit full force. The church was still reeling under the attack, bruised and debilitated but salvageable. Paul had commissioned Timothy to undertake this emergency rescue operation (1 Tim. 1:3). At the prospect of this enormous task, Timothy needed help, so Paul decided to return to Ephesus in person. The crisis in Ephesus was so serious as to cause Paul to reverse his earlier presentiment that he would not return there (Acts 20:25, 38). But fearing to be delayed, he wrote 1 Timothy in order to give his younger friend urgently needed instructions about "how people ought to conduct themselves in God's household" (1 Tim. 3:14–15). The Ephesians had misbehaved in "God's household" and abused God's welcome. The rigid measures prescribed by the apostle were especially designed to bring them back in line.

Timothy had been associated with Paul in church work for some fifteen years at the time of writing. He knew well "how people ought to conduct themselves in God's household" under normal circumstances. After all, he had been at the side of his mentor Paul in most of his travels and church planting ventures from Cilicia to Galatia, to Asia, Macedonia, and Achaia, so that the apostle could say of him, "I have no one else like him" (Phil. 2:20). But Timothy did not know yet "how people ought to conduct themselves in God's household" when the household was in a state of upheaval in the aftermath of a near fatal crash. Paul wanted to return to Ephesus to take care of the situation himself (1 Tim. 3:14; 4:13). In the meantime, Timothy was his man on the spot—and he needed all the help he could get. The letter brought the young leader instructions for providing first aid to a traumatized congregation—exceptional measures for a critical situation.

When Paul wrote to Timothy in Ephesus, the Ephesian church had been in existence for about a decade. A ministry structure had been in place during that time. Paul had seen to it that elders were appointed during the initial three years he spent there. Shortly after, he met with them at Miletus. However, that structure had proven inadequate to withstand the present crisis. A different structure was now needed in order to initiate the reconstruction phase of the Ephesian church. The remedial measures prescribed by Paul were intended to move it into convalescence.

Paul got in touch with Timothy some time prior to the writing of the letter, urging him to remain in Ephesus in order to oppose the false teachers (1:3–7). This visit would have provided him with another opportunity to instruct Timothy concerning a universally binding pattern of church leadership structure complete, with the exclusion of women—had any such thing existed at the time. In fact, it would have been unconscionable for Paul to leave his younger associate in the dark concerning such an important rule at a time when the latter was fighting for the survival of the

Ephesian church. However, the evidence suggests that Paul had never given such instructions to Timothy until he wrote this letter (3:14–15).

First Timothy itself provides the explanation for Paul's timing. During the first phase of his ministry in Ephesus, Timothy's assignment had been to silence the false teachers (1:3). Then, Paul wrote to Timothy instructing him to proceed with the reconstructive phase of his ministry in Ephesus, setting up a ministry structure that was especially designed to meet the needs of this one particular congregation at that specific point in time (2:11–3:15). The specificity of the occasion helps explain the otherwise odd exclusion from church leadership structures of all women and of all men except for married men who were also fathers of obedient and respectful children. Universalizing this structure to other congregations would have condemned the Christian church to rapid extinction worldwide.

The crisis that had befallen the Ephesian church was none other than the fulfillment of the predictions Paul had made to the elders at Miletus (Acts 20:29–30). The apostle had foreseen that false teachers, as destructive as wild beasts tearing up a flock of sheep, would decimate the congregation, and that some renegade leaders of the church could divide it. When Paul wrote 1 Timothy, his worst fears had materialized.

(2) The contents of this letter also bear witness to the gravity of the crisis that had befallen the Ephesian church. People had appeared in that city who were teaching "false doctrines," which gave way to "controversies" because they did not know what they were talking about (1 Tim. 1:3–4, 7). They had rejected "good conscience" and, as a result, they had "shipwrecked their faith." Among them, Paul handed two "over to Satan to be taught not to blaspheme" (vv. 19–20). The apostasy was so severe that he viewed it as a sign of the "later times." Indeed, some had exchanged their faith for the occult by following "deceiving spirits and things taught by demons." This insidious work was done by "hypocritical liars," whose consciences had been branded with the mark of Satan (4:1–2).

The apostate teachers had been particularly successful in spreading their false doctrine among women (5:13–15; 2 Tim. 3:6–8). Their method was to infiltrate households and gain control of spiritually unstable women, who were "always learning but never able to acknowledge the truth" (2 Tim. 3:7). Some of them had "in fact turned away to follow Satan" (1 Tim. 5:15). They themselves were propounding falsehood as they went "about from house to house . . . saying things they ought not to" (5:13). Women in Ephesus could easily gain influence since their city was both the world center for the worship of the goddess Artemis and the guardian of her image, which had allegedly fallen from heaven (Acts 19:27, 35). The temple of Artemis was recognized as one of the seven wonders of the ancient world. According to archeological evidence, it was four times the size of the Parthenon in Athens.

This influx of false teachings and of satanic influence in the Ephesian church was bound to take its toll on community life. The "controversies and quarrels" that accompanied the heresies resulted in "envy, strife, malicious talk, evil suspicions and constant friction" (1 Tim. 6:3–5). The flock was ravaged and divided, the victim of heresy and contention. Other churches, it is true, had been victimized by false teachers (e.g., Corinth, Galatia, Colosse; cf. also 2 Peter and Jude). But the virulence of the heresy compounded with the introduction of demonic doctrines and the active participation of female followers of Satan turned the Ephesian crisis into an unprecedented one among the churches established by Paul. It was a devastated congregation, whose affliction called for strong remedial prescriptions.

The churches in Crete, where Titus had been delegated as Paul's troubleshooter, were not doing much better. Although they were probably younger than the Ephesian church, they had suffered a similar crisis. The stated reason for the emergency ministry of Titus in the Cretan churches was to straighten them out and to appoint elders who conformed to Paul's specific directions (Titus 1:5). Such compliance was necessary because there were "many rebellious people, mere talkers and deceivers"

(v. 10). They had to be silenced because, like the Ephesian women who had strayed after Satan, they were "ruining whole households by teaching things they ought not to teach" (v. 11). Admittedly, they were "liars, evil brutes, lazy gluttons" (v. 12)! Their minds and "consciences [were] corrupted." They were "detestable, disobedient and unfit for doing anything good" (vv. 15–16).

From all evidence, Titus had a major problem on his hands! As in Ephesus, the heresies were taking a toll on community life. The false teachers were not only "warped and sinful . . . self-condemned" but they were also divisive persons, who should be excommunicated for generating "foolish controversies . . . arguments and quarrels" (3:9–11). Those churches were struggling in the midst of life-threatening circumstances. As in Ephesus, they faced a red alert crisis that called for exceptional measures in order to recover normalcy.

The cure proposed by the apostle to the churches at Ephesus and in Crete was commensurate with the crisis that affected them. "À *grands maux, grands moyens*"—"For great ills, strong remedies." As a great church planter and strategist, Paul could not allow those situations to deteriorate without intervening. Not only did he commission Timothy and Titus to take matters in hand, but he also gave them specific instructions to save the churches from self-destruction. Doing church as usual was out of the question.

The apostle thus proposed a plan that was dictated by a strategy of reorganization intended to curtail drastically the self-assumed ministry opportunities of the troublesome elements within these churches. This contraction of ministry would automatically isolate and eliminate the self-appointed peddlers of subversion who were disrupting the churches at Ephesus and Crete. Under the new rules, the unauthorized purveyors of heresy would be reduced to silence and their evil schemes would be thwarted. As Paul put it, "They must be silenced" (Titus 1:11). He expressly stated that he prescribed this specific ministry structure (vv. 5–9) for the purpose of counteracting the disruption that had been caused by "many rebellious people" and "deceivers," who were "ruining whole households by teaching" error for personal advantage (vv. 10–11).

Access to ministry was therefore to be withdrawn from the masses and entrusted to carefully screened individuals, reliable and loyal men with proven teaching and managerial abilities. This model was not new. The eldership was the legacy of the Jewish synagogue, itself derived from the ancient patriarchal system of government. The troops had failed; the Old Guard was called in to take over on the front line.

According to both 1 Timothy and Titus, character qualities and relational skills that normally represented all Christians exhibiting the fruit of the Spirit (Gal. 5:22–23) became, for the first time in the New Testament, the explicit requirements for leadership qualification (1 Tim. 3:2–3, 8; Titus 1:7–8). For the first time in the early church, marriage to one wife and obedient children became criteria for Christian service (1 Tim. 3:2, 4, 12; Titus 1:6). Moreover, it was ruled that a leader "must not be a recent convert" (1 Tim. 3:6), a requirement that would have disqualified ipso facto all of the elders who were normally appointed in newly planted churches (Acts 14:23). For the first time, it was explicitly specified that a leader had to "have a good reputation with outsiders" (1 Tim. 3:7). Furthermore, wives of office holders also had to be "women worthy of respect" and, like their husbands, persons of sterling character (v. 11).

In addition, a group of officers called "deacons" was identified as a separate ministry function and required specific qualifications (3:8–13). Their functions are not spelled out, but they do not seem to have been confined to "the more menial tasks of the church," as claimed by some commentators. Adherence to "the deep truths of the faith with a clear conscience" suggests a spiritual as much as a physical form of service (v. 9). In one sense, qualifications for becoming a deacon were even more stringent than for becoming an overseer/elder, since a deacon had to "first be tested" before being appointed (v. 10). For the first time in the records of the early church, office holders were appointed to their ministries only after passing a probationary test successfully. If well rendered, their deacon service, whatever it may have been, earned them "an excellent standing and great assurance in their faith in Christ Jesus" (v. 13).

The only person previously identified by name with the title "deacon" (*diakonos*) in the New Testament was a woman (Rom. 16:1; NIV translates as "servant"). The fact that in Ephesus, this ministry became restricted to married men with obedient children reveals once more the extreme measures that were taken to consolidate ministry in that church. Moreover, the fact that deacons were appointed at Ephesus and apparently not in Crete shows that church ministry structures were flexible and that they were adapted to meet local needs.

Another first-time feature of the Pastorals is that the essential duty of church leadership seems to have been the safe transmission of "sound doctrine." Because orthodoxy had been under attack by false teachers, Paul emphasized the need to safeguard the Christian tradition by passing it on as it had been received. The word "doctrine" or "teaching," which refers to the body of Christian truth under attack by the false teachers, appears fifteen times in the Pastorals against six instances in the rest of the New Testament. Not only must this body of teaching be safely passed on (cf. 2 Tim. 2:2), but there is a special focus on the protection of its integrity. The word "sound" or "wholesome" appears a dozen times in the Pastorals and only there in the New Testament as an adjective that defines the doctrine. In other words, leaders like Timothy, Titus, the overseers/elders (and possibly the deacons) were the exclusive transmitters of that "sound teaching" in Ephesus and Crete (1 Tim. 3:2, 9; 4:6, 13, 16; 5:17; 6:2–3, 14, 20; 2 Tim. 1:13–14; 2:2, 14–15, 24–25; 3:14–17; 4:2–4; Titus 1:3, 9, 13; 2:1, 10, 15; 3:8).

Also for the first time in the history of the early church, Paul did "not permit a woman to teach or to have authority over a man" (1 Tim. 2:12). Along with single men, childless married men, married men with only one child, and married men fathers of disobedient children, the Ephesian women were kept out of teaching and managerial ministries. Instead, they were to be learners "in quietness and full submission" (v. 11). In order to explain this drastic prohibition, the apostle Paul cited an illustration from the Old Testament (vv. 13–14). What happened when Ephesian women "turned away to follow Satan" (5:15) had happened once before in the Garden of Eden, when Eve followed the temptation of Satan.

Since Adam had been formed first and then Eve, God had personally instructed Adam about the tree before the creation of Eve; she had only received the instruction secondhand (Gen. 2:16–17). At temptation time, Eve would have been well-advised to stay out of it. She was, in this case, the lesser qualified to answer the devil's question. She should have deferred to Adam as the person better prepared to face Satan. Adam could not be deceived when Satan asked what God had said (3:1). He had been there and had actually heard God's instructions. Before Eve existed, he had seen God make "all kinds of trees grow" in the garden, including "the tree of life and the tree of the knowledge of good and evil" (2:8–9). The Lord God commanded him personally (in the second person singular) to eat of any tree in the garden except for the tree of knowledge of good and evil (2:16–17). Adam was the tree expert in the garden. Yet despite her disadvantage, Eve took up Satan's challenge, was deceived, and became a sinner. In the same manner, some Ephesian women had been deceived into following Satan (1 Tim. 5:15).

Fortunately for the Ephesian women, this was not the end of the story. They had been deceived, but they could now "learn in quietness" and "continue in faith, love and holiness with propriety" (2:12, 15). They were redeemable for God's purposes. God was as gracious to them as he had been to Eve when he promised her salvation through the birth of the Child, the posterity who would crush the head of the serpent tempter (2:15; cf. Gen. 3:15).

The argument in 1 Timothy 2:13–14 is not based on chronology since it draws no implication from the fact that Adam was made first—except to explain why he would not have been deceived when Eve was. Paul's use of Eve's deception as an illustration of vulnerability to error is confirmed in a parallel passage when a whole congregation, not just the women in it, is rebuked for proneness to follow false teaching (2 Cor. 11:3–6). Paul's fear is that the Corinthians may be deceived by the false teachers just "as Eve was deceived by the serpent's cunning."

The evidence in 1 Timothy 2 shows that Paul did not use the chronological precision that Adam was formed prior to Eve to draw from it a theory of Adam's "headship" over Eve. Such a notion is neither stated nor implied in Paul's reference to the creation account, nor is it stated or implied in the Genesis text. The only use Paul made of the chronological indication about Adam having been formed before Eve was to explain the fact that it was not Adam who had been deceived but Eve. What prevented Adam from being approached by Satan was the fact that he had been formed before Eve and he had been instructed directly by God about the tree. As a result, he was less vulnerable to Satan's deception than she was.

In other words, Paul's explanation was drawn from the dynamics of the Fall rather than from a theory of Adam's alleged preeminence by virtue of his chronological primacy in creation. To the contrary, Paul earlier had emphatically affirmed the irrelevance of the creation birth order for all those who are "in the Lord" (1 Cor. 11:11–12). Paul based his rationale for the prohibition of women's involvement in the Ephesian church on the dynamics of Eve's temptation, not on any doctrine of her alleged inferiority in having been created after Adam.

Because Eve was created after Adam and because, having been deceived in the Fall, she became a transgressor, the alternative absolutist interpretation would require that no woman could ever teach or have authority over men. This role would be assigned exclusively to men. This would mean, however, that Calvary and Pentecost make no difference to the status of female subordination that had allegedly developed because of the Fall. In other words, the cross of Jesus could not release sufficient grace to reverse the disgrace presumably brought upon all women by Eve's offense. This would also mean that because Adam was made first, all believing men may receive release from their consequences of the Fall (Gen. 3:17–19) through the redemptive work of Christ; but that redemptive work would fail to lift the legacy of guilt that believing women would allegedly continue to inherit from Eve's actions in the Garden. In other words, the death and resurrection of Jesus Christ do not have the power to make all things new for women, to reverse the effects of the Fall and to achieve a new creation. Indeed, some churchmen seem to be willing to reduce Christianity to the status of a gender religion, complete with a divinity controlled by maleness both within his nature and in the realm of his creational and redemptive priorities.

The negative theological implications for the doctrine of redemption of the absolutist position regarding the prohibition of 1Timothy 2:11–15 are too devastating to contemplate. Interpreting this passage as an argument for any continuing effects among believers of the primacy of Adam and of the sinfulness of Eve voids the cross of its redemptive and renewing power. If, however, Paul's reference to Adam and Eve is properly interpreted as an illustration of what happens when unqualified people take over, it acquires a direct bearing on the situation that the apostle was trying to correct at Ephesus when he required female propounders of error to quit teaching and dominating men, to start learning right doctrine quietly, to tend to their families, and to cultivate their devotional lives.

Moreover, should the reference to Adam and Eve in 1 Timothy 2:11–15 be interpreted as Eve's violation of an alleged hierarchical order between her and Adam, men would have even less right than women to teach. According to verse 14, Eve's offense was not usurping authority but only being deceived, as a result of which she, as an individual, became a transgressor. Adam, however, committed the infinitely greater offense of violating the hierarchical order between God and himself, which order had been revealed to him personally in the prohibition about the tree (Gen. 2:16–17). According to Scriptures, the result of his offense is not limited just to himself. He is the one who brought sin and death into the world, not only upon himself but for the whole human race (Rom. 5:14; 1 Cor. 15:22). Both the offense and the consequences are biblically described as being infinitely more grievous in the case of Adam than for Eve. Should Paul's prohibition to teach be interpreted as punishment for bucking authority, men should have been barred from teaching before women were. Instead, Paul's point about Adam and Eve was that unqualified people should not do ministry; they should learn first in order to become qualified.

The story of creation and the Fall was not new for the Apostle. Had the prohibition for women to teach been based on a theory of the authority of Adam over Eve because of his chronological primacy or on the impropriety of all Christian women to teach because of Eve's transgression at the Fall, it would have required universal enforcement. There would have been no reason for the apostle to wait until nearly the end of his life to make it known. All the churches that Paul had established from the beginning of his ministry should have been informed about this important ruling. The Ephesian church should have been informed of it ten years earlier. Timothy, who had worked faithfully at Paul's side, should have been informed of it fifteen years earlier.

The very wording of Paul's prohibition indicates its novelty as a response to the emergency in Ephesus. Paul assumed personal responsibility for it at the time of writing: "I do not permit. . . ." He was not referring to a universal rule that might have prevailed in Ephesus as in all churches and that the Ephesian women had broken. He offered no rebuke for women having allegedly violated church order by engaging in teaching when they were not supposed. There was no reprimand for disregarding preexistent restrictions to ministry. Paul's prohibition was just that—a Holy Spirit-inspired prohibition for the women *of Ephesus* at the time of writing. The New Testament offers no universally applicable rule or a general policy known and practiced in all the churches on this issue. Paul's statement was a temporary restraint, of the same order as all men being barred from leadership ministries except for married men with obedient, respectful, and believing children. Such restrictions on women and men were needed in order to save the churches in Ephesus and Crete from self-destruction.

Of course, it could be argued that the apostle Paul was given late in his career a new revelation about ecclesiastical offices that was applicable to all churches. In a process of progressive revelation, he was now given new insights about church order, which he was in turn sharing with Timothy.

But evidence in 1 Timothy militates against such a theory. Paul had originally intended to convey those instructions to Timothy directly, through the means of oral communication by going to Ephesus in person (1 Tim. 3:14). Orders intended to be given by word of mouth to one local church could hardly have been designed to carry universal relevance for all churches at all times. The reason Paul gave for writing down his instructions was for Timothy to receive them urgently in case his own projected trip to Ephesus should be delayed (v. 15). There is no evidence that Paul took any steps to disseminate his "I do not permit a woman to teach" decision to any church other than to Ephesus, or that God authorized this prohibition to be absolutized as a universal canon for all times.

It should also be noted that the instructions about church order that Paul sent to Titus for the churches in Crete were written during the same period of time as 1 Timothy. Yet not only the prohibition for women to teach is absent from the letter to Titus, but the opposite is true. Titus was instructed by Paul to teach older women so that they could become literally "teachers-of-what-is-good" (Titus 2:3). The Christian women of Crete were apparently not propounding apostasy as their Ephesian counterparts were doing. Therefore, the prohibition was not extended to them. Women were forbidden to teach in Ephesus, but in Crete some were trained to teach others (see my *Beyond Sex Roles*, pp. 176–77). It is difficult to imagine a stronger proof for the specificity of the 1 Timothy prohibition.

The process of progressive revelation requires that truth revealed subsequently be in line with prior truth and fulfill it (Matt. 5:17). However, in the case of the prohibition to women in 1 Timothy 2, there is no progression but contradiction and even regression from one kind of truth to its opposite. The movement of regression was from a polity that required leaders to equip, support, and facilitate congregation-based ministries to a system that required leaders to take over ministries, a shift from support roles of leaders as coaches and tutors to Old Testament patterns of leader monopoly on ministry.

When later truth contradicts prior truth, it becomes a case of exception—not progressive revelation. An example of this principle may be cited, among many, from the first pages of the New Testament. The Gospel of Matthew makes it clear that when Jesus began preaching in Galilee, his ministry was to include Gentiles. He first proclaimed the nearness of the kingdom in an area called "Galilee of the Gentiles," to the people who sat in darkness in the land of the shadow of death but who saw a great light (Matt. 4:13–17). However, when Jesus sent his disciples on their first preaching mission, he strictly ordered them not to go among the Gentiles but to confine their ministry to Israel. He also forbade them to secure any financial support for their missionary endeavor and to take any baggage for their travel—not even a change of clothes (10:5–10).

Should this teaching that concerned a limited, short-term missionary endeavor be isolated and absolutized as the model for contemporary missionary work, it would lead to disaster. This teaching is not a case of progressive revelation but an exception that stands in sharp contrast to the normative New Testament teaching about the missionary outreach of the church. It must be interpreted in reference to its own historical contingencies. Basing Christian doctrine and practice on cases of exception instead of normative, well-attested scriptural teaching can easily lead to confusion and error.

The rigid concentration of ministry reflected in the Pastoral Letters and the fastidious precautions stipulated by Paul for ecclesiastical appointments in Crete and more so at Ephesus show how badly he had been burned by the dysfunction that had affected those churches. This time around, as he tried to reclaim them, Paul was taking no chances. He made sure that only people with unassailable qualifications could access ministry. Others would learn in quietness and submission, pray, and do good deeds, until such time as the churches would have healed enough to resume normal life with full participation of the constituency in ministry. In Paul's own words, "All who cleanse themselves of the things I have mentioned will become special utensils, dedicated and useful to the owner of the house, ready for every good work" (2 Tim. 2:21 NRSV).

With the instructions of 1 Timothy, Paul was attempting to rescue the church from apostasy and help it to function eventually as authentic community. The apostle had seen right. One generation later, history bore witness to the fact that the Ephesian church made the expected comeback. The Lord sent them a letter through the apostle John to commend them for their perseverance in the face of the hardships that they had endured in order to remain faithful. In particular, the Lord congratulated the Ephesian Christians for having been able to identify the false apostles in their midst and to denounce them as evildoers (Rev. 2:2–3).

The remedy had been painful and the recovery was not yet complete. The downfall had been so great that lost ground was not totally regained. The past turmoils of the church and, possibly, the severe but necessary restrictions instituted by Paul had caused the community's love to grow cold. But the Lord was still with the church, walking "among the seven golden lampstands" (Rev. 2:1) and challenging it to become again authentic community by returning to the loving relationships of the beginning (vv. 4–5). Thus, the Scripture confirms that Paul's strategy to reclaim Ephesus had met with measured success. The church had come out of the dark side of community to walk toward the sunlight of oneness.

As illustrated by the diverse fortunes of the Ephesian church, a structure of ministry may vary, depending on the circumstances and the needs of a local church at different stages of its development. The notable differences between the definition of ministry at Ephesus and in Crete, churches to which Paul wrote at the same point in time, show that structures of ministry may also vary from church to church, depending on their particular needs and circumstances. The church at Ephesus needed deacons; there were none in Crete. The overseers/elders in Ephesus were not to be recent converts; no such restriction is mentioned for Crete. For most New Testament churches, gender, marital, and parental status were not raised as an issue for becoming leaders; according to the Pastorals, only "blameless" married men with obedient and believing children could become leaders. Not only common sense and the experience of the corporate world but also Scripture shows that rigid and uniform structures of organization stifle community, whereas flexible and adaptable forms of organization promote participation, ownership, and growth.

There are abundant biblical data to show that the New Testament churches moved on a continuum between two opposite models, both biblical. The normative model at one end of the continuum called for structures of ministry that were open, participatory, and based on spiritual gifts. The function of leaders was to equip and support congregation-based ministries. As noted in the foregoing survey, most of the New Testament churches tended to move in that direction.

The other model was remedial. It is represented by the ministry structures of the Pastorals, which were highly selective and restricted exclusively to married men with obedient and believing children. The function of those leaders was to control an unruly congregation and to "direct the affairs of the church" in order to bring them back to order. This contingent model is in the Scriptures, and it may not be dismissed as an ancient cultural phenomenon that has no relevance for today.

Any church that finds itself in a situation similar to the churches in Ephesus or Crete is duty-bound to abide by this model of church order, although the test for the recruitment of managerial competency may be more sophisticated today than the running of an orderly household. The criteria for proven managerial qualities may not always be determined on the basis of family status and gender, yet the underlying biblical principle remains valid: Whenever a church faces a life-threatening crisis, access to ministry should be restricted to the best qualified individuals. For sick churches, applying the context-specific prescriptions of the remedial model may be their only hope to become healthy and to move, as did the Ephesian church, toward the normative model. Unfortunately, church situations may still occur today that require the institution of this religious equivalent to martial law.

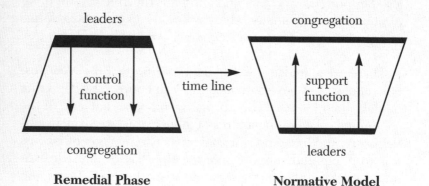

Remedial Phase   **Normative Model**

This is not a novel approach. The Scriptures contain many other instructions that are likewise context-specific and applicable only within circumstances that justify them. Several examples are available in 1 Timothy alone. This letter contains a strong command for slaves "to consider their masters worthy of full respect" (1 Tim. 6:1–2). This injunction prescribed a certain mode of conduct for Christian slaves wherever they may have been found. However, the text may not be used to absolutize the social context of slavery and to claim that the Bible supports the institution of slavery.

The apostle Paul advised Timothy to use wine because of its digestive virtues (5:23). This command may have validity in some contexts, but it may not be universalized to current application so that wine becomes the Christian medical prescription for all stomach pains and other "frequent illnesses."

The church of Ephesus ran a welfare program for needy widows over sixty years old (5:3–16). The letter contains detailed instructions for the administration of this program. While a similar program may have been operative in the Jerusalem church (Acts 6:1), there is no evidence that it existed in other early churches or that it must be forced on contemporary churches simply because it was the rule in Ephesus.

The apostle Paul gave an amazing teaching in connection with his prohibition about women. He wrote that since Eve became a sinner after being deceived, she (or women) "will be saved through childbearing" (1 Tim. 2:15). This teaching is even more binding than the prohibition itself. It has the force of a universal premise, whereas the prohibition was formulated as a personal command that pertained to an immediate situation, "I do not permit. . . ." Moreover, the case from Eve's deception was used as a supportive context for the prohibition by way of an illustration from the Old Testament. However, the teaching about salvation through childbearing is a conclusion directly connected to the creation story (v. 14). It is a categorical statement of fact and cannot be viewed as an illustration.

Should the statement about women not teaching be absolutized, the teaching about female salvation through childbearing must be treated with equal rigor, must be interpreted with the same literalism, and must be promulgated as a universal rule. Consistency would then require that everything the Scripture teaches about salvation by grace through faith be set aside for half of the population, and that it be replaced with the doctrine that women are saved by having babies. Considerable support could be marshaled for this view from biblical passages that deal with infertility. Accordingly, all women would be excluded from teaching ministries, and all childless women would be excluded from salvation.

It is, however, evident from the contents of 1 Timothy that Paul was addressing cases of exception. As outlined above, the women of Ephesus had no small part in the intense disorders that had disrupted their church. It was important for the apostle that they be brought under discipline—like most of their male counterparts who were also restricted from teaching. Once restored, they would "continue in faith, love and holiness with propriety" (v. 15).

With the same firmness as for the prohibition for women to teach, Paul also forbade the Ephesian women to wear braided hair, gold, pearls, or expensive clothes (2:9–10). There may be contemporary situations that require strict adherence to such rules because of social and religious contexts similar to that of Ephesus. But absolutizing this passage as a universal rule for all times instead of determining its applicability context would mean that all Christian women should walk today with their hair loose, stripped of jewelry, and in clothes purchased at the neighborhood thrift store. While this may work for some, others might find it to be a counterproductive way of expressing their Christian identity.

The same principles apply to the Pastorals' instructions concerning ministry structures. Those instructions remain as valid today as when they were first given to the churches in Ephesus and Crete. But their contemporary point of application is for churches that find themselves in a condition similar to that of the churches in Ephesus and Crete. Otherwise, lifting those prescriptions for church order out of the Bible, absolutizing them as if they were the only model for ministry and leadership found in the New Testament, and applying them to all churches, sick or not, is a sure-fire method for making them all sick. Contemporary churches that keep pushing services and programs instead of building biblically-defined community, and churches that struggle on the edge of survival instead of crushing the gates of hell may well ponder whether their ministry structures are patterned after the appropriate biblical model.

"Bible-believing" churches should be especially careful not to fall into patterns of selective application of the ecclesiastical order prescribed in the Pastorals. Partial obedience is no obedience. When they decide to adopt any of those prescriptions, those churches obligate themselves, for the sake of consistency and integrity, to follow them all.

An American church leader has made this claim: "First Timothy 2:11–12 clearly states that women are not to teach or have authority over men, and 1 Timothy 3:1–13 continues with an immediate application of this teaching to the offices of the church." This leader is willing to interpret to the letter and absolutize the instructions about women, but he conveniently glosses over the instructions given about men in 3:1–13. This text requires that men who hold office be married and have believing children who are also obedient and respectful. Strict adherence to this one clause has the potential to disqualify many men who hold office in contemporary churches and to decimate ecclesiastical leadership structures. Moreover, the same texts also require that all men who hold office be above reproach, temperate, self-controlled, respectable, hospitable, able to teach, not given to drunkenness, not violent but gentle, not quarrelsome, not lovers of money, blameless, not overbearing, not quick-tempered, not pursuing dishonest gain, upright, holy, disciplined, and able to encourage by sound doctrine and to refute those who oppose it, and that they have a good reputation with outsiders (3:2–3; Titus 1:7–9).

One can easily understand the reluctance of present-day church leaders to enforce the strict requirements that the Pastorals lay on male leadership. The cumulative effect of the imposition on contemporary churches of such specifications would be disastrous for them. It would annihilate a great deal of their leadership by disqualification, wipe out their ministry structures, and condemn huge numbers of churches to extinction. It would also throw into a horrible dilemma spiritually gifted men who do not have a call to marriage (1 Cor. 7:1, 7–8, 25–27, 32–34). They would either remain single, suppress their spiritual gifts, and betray their call to ministry, or they would force themselves into marriage and try to raise obedient children in order to qualify for ministry.

To insist on the rigorous application of the clause for women while glossing over any of the stringent specifications of the clause for men is to practice what the Scriptures describe as "favoritism" and "committing sin" (James 2:9). For those who choose to follow the remedial structural model of the Pastorals, neither clause is optional. They belong together. They are equally binding for women and men, and they tolerate no exceptions.

Some time ago, I received a long distance call from a woman whom I will call Ann. She was seeking my advice as the author of *Beyond Sex Roles*. She explained that a new pastor, recently graduated from a large seminary in the south of the United States, had come to the church of which she was a member. The pastor had started a couples' Bible study class, which she and her husband attended and enjoyed. However, when her husband's work schedule changed, she decided to go to the class by herself. As she came to the door, she explained her husband's absence to the pastor. He refused to let her continue with the class because, according to him, it was not right for her to advance spiritually beyond her "leader" husband.

Ann knew of a group of women from the church who were meeting informally for Bible study and prayer. She decided to join them. A few weeks later, the pastor showed up at one of their sessions. With Bible in hand, he declared that, according to 1 Timothy 2:12, women were forbidden to teach and that the group would have to disband unless they could secure a male teacher or place the group under male sponsorship. After some discussion, the pastor agreed to submit the matter to the church's all-male board of elders, who concurred with his decision.

Soon after, the pastor noticed that all but three of the Sunday School teachers were female. He and the elders decided that, in obedience to Scripture, the female teachers would have to be replaced or supervised by male teachers. Since none were found, some classes were consolidated under the three male teachers and the rest were shut down. Several families within the church then asked that the issue be brought to a congregational meeting. In anticipation of this discussion, the pastor and the elders decided that since their Bible text forbade a woman "to have authority over a man" (1 Tim. 2:12) and since casting a vote could be viewed as an exercise of authority, the women present at the congregational meeting would be exempted from voting.

It was at this point that Ann was calling me for advice. I told her that the decisions of the pastor and elders were totally consistent with literal adherence to the one verse of Scripture they were claiming as guidance for their church, since this particular text, followed to the letter, ruled out female involvement in teaching and forbade women to exercise authority over men.

"But," Ann exclaimed, "they are ruining our church. There won't be anything left of it." I then asked Ann if her pastor was married. He was. I asked if he had any children. He had none. I told Ann, "I feel sorry for your church because, in addition to all your troubles, you will also lose your pastor. He obviously will have to resign." I showed her that the same biblical passage that the pastor and the elders were using against women set severe character stipulations for men who could teach, preach, lead, serve, or manage the church. I especially pointed out the requirement stated in 1 Timothy 3:3–5 that any such man must be married and be the father of children old enough to demonstrate obedience and respect as proof of their father's competence to do ministry. I also noted that such children must be of sufficient age to profess personal faith and lead self-disciplined lives for their father to qualify for ministry (Titus 1:6).

I went on to ask her how many of the men on the board of elders met this biblical criterion. She went through their names and concluded that only one out of seven did—more or less. To this I answered, "Ann, again I am sorry for your church. The elders have ruled themselves out of legitimacy. They will also have to resign." As this realization sunk in, there was a long period of silence on the line. Finally, she whispered, "I see." She added, "Now I know what we must do." She thanked me and I never heard from her again.

During the last twenty years, numerous books and articles have been published and innumerable sermons preached, calling for the rigorous enforcement of ministry restrictions on women as per 1 Timothy 2:11–12. However, their authors never show the same enthusiasm for an equally rigid implementation of the provisions that pertain to men within the very next paragraph of this letter (3:1–13). It can be easily verified that many authors and many churchmen absolutize the provisions that pertain to women in 1 Timothy 2, giving them a universal field of application, while they refuse to deal with explicit biblical instructions that require male leaders to be married and to manage competently a household that comprises obedient and believing children. Such people must be called to accountability for the deception involved in the practice of the double standard—which practice the Bible condemns as discriminating among yourselves and becoming judges with evil thoughts (James 2:4).

The biblical test of true community is very practical. The body is a unit; though it is made of many parts, it functions as one body. The body is complete and healthy when each part functions optimally, in harmony with the other parts. The mark of authentic community is full participation of its members in the ministry of the community. Oneness cannot happen when parts of the body are paralyzed into inaction by ugly discriminations. The atrophy or impairment of one part of the body can cripple the whole body (1 Cor. 12:26). But oneness blooms with full effervescence in the heat of joyful and generous teamwork when each part of the body pours all that it is into the building and expansion of community. Then community can become what God intends it to be—not a crippled body but "a radiant church, without stain or wrinkle or any other blemish, but holy and blameless" (Eph. 5:27).

CHAPTER FOUR

Leadership

Community doesn't just happen. Its creation and preservation require much hard work. The recrudescence at the end of the twentieth century of narrow nationalisms and of devastating religious and tribal fanaticisms is tearing apart long-established communal societies around the globe. The breakdown of community plunges whole regions into chaos and threatens world peace. All it takes to ignite the fires of divisive intolerance and of murderous exclusiveness is one loudmouth spouting off slogans of hatred and prejudice. However, the maintenance of community requires intentionality, perseverance, and sacrifice.

It might seem that, because of the shared spiritual allegiances and of the indwelling presence of the Holy Spirit, community would happen effortlessly among Christians as the natural by-product of deep spiritual commitments. According to Scripture, Christians should be transformed by the renewing of their minds (Rom. 12:2). This means that they should be engaged together in a process of change that drives them away from patterns of behavior detrimental to community building and that compels them to band together to re-create oneness (vv. 3–5).

Unfortunately, the pressure to conform to the patterns of this world is difficult to resist. The challenge of the gospel for Christians is to establish contrast communities that present kingdom alternatives to the world. However, this makes demands that often seem to be too radical. It becomes easier to slip into the security of conformity to the ways of ambient cultures. From the beginning, the pull has been from freedom in Christ to regression under yokes of slavery. But Christ is never willing to abandon his church.

In order to guide God's people in the ways of authentic community, he gave some to be apostles, evangelists, pastors, teachers, bishops, elders, and deacons—people appointed to serve the body of Christ so that community could be built up and protected. Such ministries or variations of them provide the elements that constitute the leadership systems of local churches.

From the survey conducted in the previous chapter, it is evident that the New Testament does not prescribe one particular leadership system to fit uniformly all churches. Different needs and different circumstances call for different forms of governance. It appears from the biblical record that all the churches had elders but with various degrees of visibility. In addition, the Jerusalem church had apostles. In Philippi, there were both overseers and deacons, but both groups seemed to be inconspicuous. At a later stage in the life of the Ephesian church, Paul established deacons, but they seem absent in the churches of Crete. In both Ephesus and Crete, elder candidates had to meet rigorous standards in order to qualify for their position. These went unspecified in other New Testament letters.

Despite such variations, the New Testament definition of leadership includes three essential features that remain constant for all churches: *Leadership is a servant ministry, based on spiritual gifts and always plural.* These components of leadership, biblically defined, will be discussed in that order. Since the latter two are a function of the first, they will be treated briefly.

A. SERVANT LEADERSHIP

Because Jesus knew that the kingdom he was bringing was not of this world, he also knew that it would not be structured like the kingdoms of this world. Early in his ministry, he made it clear that his kingdom would be for the poor in spirit, the meek, and the merciful. But his disciples lived in a world where these sorts of people were ruthlessly crushed at the bottom of the pyramid of hierarchies that made up their social environments.

The pecking order was an inescapable reality of daily life, whether in the home, at the marketplace, in the synagogue, or in political life; everyone had to assume one's appropriate rank on multiple ladders of hierarchy in consideration of birth, race, gender, fortune, and influence. This mentality was so pervasive that the disciples could not think of the kingdom of God in different terms. They knew that Jesus was dedicated to the task of launching a new community. They also realized that they would be the charter members of this organization. Because they were the first participants, they also thought that they should be foremost in it. But there were twelve of them, and all twelve of them could not be in first place. So, they argued among themselves as to "who was the greatest" (Mark 9:33–34). They were in competition against each other for the position of front-runner in the kingdom of Jesus Christ!

When Jesus learned of the disciples' contest, he sat down. Their discussion was a hard blow to him, and he took it sitting down. Gathering the Twelve for an emergency teaching session, he summarized his message in the following words: "If anyone wants to be first, he must be the very last, and the servant of all" (9:35).

Jesus did not condemn as wrong the desire to be first. Leaders are needed, and the desire to use one's gift of leadership is legitimate. But Jesus transformed the concept of leadership by redefining its style and the motivation for doing it. The style demands that roles of leadership be fulfilled not with the pride of one who comes first, not with the self-glory of one who wins a competition, but with the humility of one who comes in last. The motivation should not be the desire to rule, control, or command, but to support and assist others, just as a servant does.

In other words, leadership among Christians is not authority-intensive but service-based. Biblical leadership is willingness to fall behind in order to help those who are struggling instead of striving to be first and to win the competition for power. There is no command or instruction in the New Testament for any Christian to exercise authority over another. But there are strict orders for all Christians, including leaders, to act as servants within their communities (Matt. 20:26; Mark 9:35; Gal. 5:13; etc.).

In order to drive the point home, Jesus gave the disciples a living illustration of what it means to be servant to others. He brought "a little child" and had him stand in their midst, and then he took the child in his arms (Mark 9:36). The disciples had no use for children. They treated them as a nuisance and wanted them out of their way (10:13–16). But Jesus showed them the deep meaning of servanthood by making a child, who had no significance for the disciples, the most important person in the world for him at that moment. Jesus explained to them that by loving and serving lesser ones, as he was doing for the child, they would really be serving Christ and loving God, who had sent him to serve in this manner (9:37).

Jesus went on to reveal the servant-mindedness that motivates the Godhead by stating that he was willing to identify with the lowly child as closely as he was himself identified with the Father. By receiving children one received him, just as one who received him also received the Father. This was a complete reversal of the competitive, ascendancy-driven values of the world. It meant going all the way down the world's ladders of hierarchy and lifting up those at the bottom above oneself. Concern for children, for the weak, and for the disadvantaged was not invented by welfare organizations. It was ordained by Jesus as an authentic expression of servant leadership (Matt. 25:34–40).

The disciples seemed to be bent on going out of their way to demonstrate how uncomprehending they were of Jesus' teaching and of the ways of the kingdom of God. Not long after this teaching, Jesus caught them chasing away parents who wanted him to bless their children (Mark 10:13–16). Jesus became "indignant" and told the bumptious disciples, driven by upward mobility aspirations, that unless they became as submissive and unpretentious as the little children they were despising, they would have no part in the kingdom of God. In order to enter that kingdom, they had to receive it as a child does (v. 15). A child receiving the kingdom does not aspire to positions of authority and power. The kingdom is not for those who use it to position themselves above others but for those who enter it as servants.

1. Downward Mobility

The worst was yet to come. On previous occasions, Jesus had caught the disciples in situations of infraction to his teaching as they were competing among themselves for positions of preeminence. But a short time after they had tried to push the children away, two of them came out in the open. James and John, the Zebedee brothers, set aside all pretense and, with their mother, approached Jesus privately to obtain a favor from him (Matt. 20:20–28). Their outrageous request was for the best seats in the kingdom. They conceived of God's kingdom as a pyramid of power within which they would occupy the top positions, so as to be second only to Christ and to share in his authority and preeminence.

In response, Jesus offered them a complete reversal of the morbid values they had espoused; he had only a cup of suffering and self-sacrifice to share with them. They were dreaming of upward mobility; all he could offer them was downward mobility. And to show by the way of personal example that he understood his own function of kingdom sovereignty in terms of submission and service, he deferred the brothers' request to his Father's authority, unwilling to presume of it himself (vv. 22–23). He had come as a servant to give his life as a ransom on the cross—not to distribute positions of authority. By asking Jesus for places at his right hand and at his left hand, the two brothers were unwittingly asking to be crucified with him on either side of him.

That the mentality exhibited by the two brothers was shared by all the disciples became evident when they "became indignant with the two brothers" upon learning of their request (v. 24). Just prior to this incident, Jesus had described his ministry to them in terms of sacrifice, suffering, and death (vv. 17–19). However, they could not hear him because they were all dreaming of positions of power and glory. So, the ten other disciples became angry because the two brothers had gotten to Jesus first with their candidacy for the positions of highest prestige and authority.

Ever patient, Jesus gathered again all the disciples and launched into another teaching session to lay down in unmistakable terms the principles for the practice of authority and leadership in the new community (vv. 25–28). This teaching was not just about the desire to be great or greatest but especially about jockeying for positions of power and "exercising authority." Elsewhere Jesus gave vast amounts of instructions on community life and interpersonal relations among believers. But he said very little about community organization proper. Since this is his main teaching on the subject, it is worth pondering and taking it to heart.

Jesus cited two models of governance—one that capitalizes on the use of authority as the principle of community organization and the other that bases community organization on the principle of mutual servanthood. Although these two paradigms are antithetical to each other, Jesus presented both as having legitimacy, albeit in different realms of application.

The first model cited by Jesus was so prevalent that it required little explanation. Everyone living within the Roman empire was well acquainted with it. The imperial administration of Rome was constructed as a well-ordered hierarchy, over which the emperor ruled as supreme authority. Jesus described this system as rulers exercising lordship over the people and high officials exercising authority over them (v. 25). Jesus never questioned the legitimacy of this system. He was himself subject to the rule of government (17:24–27), and he advocated obedient recognition of the rights of the state (22:21). He knew that a fallen world could not survive the downward pull of chaos without solid authority structures. The only exception admitted by Jesus concerned cases when the political power idolatrously substituted itself for God—when Caesar usurped what belonged to God (22:21). When this actually happened, followers of Jesus felt obligated to obey God rather than human beings (Acts 5:29). Otherwise, they maintained the legitimacy of civil authority and insisted on the necessity for Christians to submit to it (Rom. 13:1–7; 1 Tim. 2:1–2; Titus 3:1; 1 Peter 2:13–17).

As the kingdom alternative to the world's obsession with authority structures, Jesus introduced the opposite model, with an emphatically negative command that rejected the hierarchical, authority-intensive model he had just cited. Literally rendered, his command was: "Not so [will it be] with you" (Matt. 20:26). While Jesus acknowledged the right of the rulers of this world to exercise authority over their subjects, he categorically ruled out any such practice within the Christian community.

At one fell swoop, Jesus unequivocally rejected the hierarchical model as the basis for communal organization among Christians and replaced it with an alternative contrast model of downward mobility, patterned on his own itinerary of humiliation from the highest glory to the lowest condition as crucified Savior (Matt. 20:26–28). It is paradoxical that some contemporary church leaders vehemently oppose strong government in the political realm where, according to the New Testament, it is most needed (Rom. 13:3–4, 6–7), but then turn around and insist on rigid hierarchical structures for communities of faith where, according to the New Testament, they are the least needed.

Jesus described the driving force behind Christian community structuring as the obligation of each to become "servant" and even "slave" to the group. He replaced imperial rulership with the imperative of servanthood, and the love of power with the power of love. Because Jesus knew that his disciples had no precedent and no model to grasp the nature of servant leadership, he cited one absolute indisputable and unequivocal example of servant leadership: his own. He was the supreme Lord, but he became the archetypal servant. Likewise, instead of seeking to lord it over each other, his followers must be servants to each other.

Servant leadership has more to do with the *attitude* of leaders than with church polity. Some churches, groups of churches, or denominational associations that are constituted on a hierarchical pattern are led by humble, servant-minded leaders, who use their position to empower others into ministry rather than to lord it over them. There are other churches that have congregational forms of governance calling for openness and participation, but all too often such congregations are ruled by strong individuals or by a coterie of dominant individuals, who have wrested for themselves the authority and the ministry that belong to their constituencies. With the right spirit, hierarchical structures can be made the instrument of servanthood just as democratically constituted bodies can fall victim to abuse at the hands of power-driven individuals. Ultimately, the attitude with which leadership is approached is more determinant to the life of a community than the formal definitions of its constitutional status.

The insistence of Jesus on servanthood as the mode of leadership among Christians does not mean that he was against authority. He himself claimed to have absolute authority, and he was not loath to use it, especially to subdue evil powers. He also recognized the legitimacy of political power, and he submitted to the authority of the state.

Moreover, as servant head of the church, he reserves sole ownership over it and is jealously protective of his bride. The only delegate he ever authorized to exercise authority over the church on his behalf is the Paraclete, the Holy Spirit, who indwells each believer and thus provides corporate guidance to the body (John 16:12–15). When, at the end of his earthly ministry and before ascending to heaven, Jesus commissioned the Eleven to make disciples of all nations, he made it clear that he was keeping strict monopoly on his authority (Matt. 28:16–20). He authorized them to teach what he had commanded them. They were only transmitting agents; they could not arrogate for themselves the authority that belongs to him alone.

Eventually, the substance of what Jesus commanded his disciples to teach was couched in writing and became incorporated in Scripture. Today, no teacher or leader may claim for himself or herself the authority that belongs to the written Word. As human agents for the transmission of that Word, leaders have no authority of their own apart from their dependency on Scripture. Inasmuch as they interpret the Scriptures accurately, they may become authoritative (not authoritarian!) in their teaching. But the authority remains in the Scripture. It belongs to God alone.

At the defining moment when Jesus ruled out the use of authority as an option for the structuring of his community, he cited his own example of suffering servant as the model for the relations of mutual submission that were to prevail among his followers (Matt. 20:26–28). In total servanthood, he was giving "his life as a ransom for many." This linkage between Christ's definition of the nature of the new community and the statement about his redemptive ministry to the world was not accidental. Christ knew that the purpose of his mission on earth was to bring redemption to individual souls in order to bond them together into the eternal community. He came as a servant Savior to form a community of servants.

The whole sweep of the history of redemption as recorded in Scripture tells of God's endeavors to obtain the salvation of individual human beings. Because lostness is primarily an individual condition, salvation must also be personally experienced. But the Scriptures also teach that God's ultimate purpose is to gather the redeemed into communities where they can grow and serve through their integration into the fellowship of God's people.

Jesus recognized this duality when he described his mission. On one hand, he viewed himself as the good shepherd who lays down his life for the sheep (John 10:11). But on the other, he was also the shepherd of the flock because "there shall be one flock and one shepherd" (v. 16). Christ's concern is for both the saving of individuals and the forming of the community. He is Savior and Shepherd.

When King Herod inquired from the religious leaders of his day where the Christ was to be born, they cited to him the Old Testament prophecy that pointed to Bethlehem and predicted the coming of a "ruler who will be the shepherd of my people Israel" (Matt. 2:3–6). As the angel Gabriel appeared to Mary and announced to her the forthcoming birth of "the Son of the Most High," he quickly explained the purpose of his mission: "The Lord God will give him the throne of his father David, and he will reign over the house of Jacob forever; his kingdom will never end" (Luke 1:32–33). And when the time came for the hosts of angels to celebrate the birth of the Christ child, they gave glory to God as they anticipated the birth of the new community, "Glory to God in the highest, and on earth peace to [those] on whom his favor rests" (2:14). From before his birth, Jesus was designated as the heavenly King who came to earth as Savior to redeem sinners, in order to build them into a new community he would cherish, just as a man loves his bride.

Jesus knew the sad history of community on earth. He taught about the goodness of God's creation "at the beginning," when God formed the original community of oneness (Matt. 19:4–6). But he also spoke of a usurper who claimed to be the ruler of this world (John 12:31) and who "was a murderer from the beginning" (8:44). Jesus saw it as his own mission to reclaim for God the community that had been hijacked by the devil at the Fall. The ruler of the world had debased God's community of oneness by branding it with his own trademark of rulership: the arrogation by the creature of personal sovereignty over other creatures—sovereignty that belongs to the Creator alone (Gen. 3:16).

As God's counteroffensive, Christ was now establishing his own contrast community. Satan's signature on his pseudo-communities was the ruler who kept subjects under his control. The hallmark of new community was the servant who lifted up other people. Satan had brought in rulership; Christ was restoring mutual submission. Ubiquitous structures of authority barely held the ancient world together; mutual servanthood provided the impetus for the church to conquer the ancient world through the power of love. The servant ministry of him who gave his life as a ransom for many was to create an alternative community of servants in a world that cringed helplessly under the heavy foot of rulership.

The disciples, however, were so immersed in their world of unbridled hierarchy that they never understood what Christ meant by servanthood until after the crucifixion. On the evening before his death, as they gathered for their last meal together, no servant showed up to perform the traditional foot-washing. It never occurred to any of the disciples to take upon himself the role of that servant, if not to one another, at least for the Master. Instead, Jesus was the one who stooped at their feet with a basin and towel to burn into their memory a haunting lesson of the meaning of servanthood that they could never forget (John 13:1–17).

2. Consensual Decision-Making

To prepare the disciples as pioneer builders of the new community, Jesus also gave them instructions relative to the decision-making process in the community of servants. In a hierarchical society, the person in charge makes the decisions for the group. Not so according to Jesus and his model for community. As a case in point, Jesus evoked the unfortunate but commonplace occurrence of a believer wronging another believer (Matt. 18:15–20). In a traditional setting, the contention would ultimately be resolved by submitting it to the authority figure of the group, who would rule on its behalf. But in the process outlined by Jesus, no authority structure was designated to settle the issue, except for the group itself.

In a first step, the offended party must approach the offender, not as a judge or an accuser, but for the purpose of bringing the other person to reason and to achieve reconciliation (v. 15). The purpose of this process is to serve the best interest of all concerned: one servant extending forgiveness to an erring fellow servant in the best interests of the whole community.

Should this first confrontation remain unproductive, the case is still not submitted to some preestablished authority structure. Instead, the group ministers to itself as one or two witnesses recruited by the aggrieved party become involved to vouch for the integrity of the process (v. 16). Finally, the matter is brought before the church for a final decision (v. 17). Remarkably, this procedure dispenses totally with an authority structure that manages the life of the congregation from above it. The decision-making process is self-contained.

It is noteworthy that this teaching was given to the disciples in the context of their question about "who is the greatest in the kingdom of heaven" (Matt. 18:1). This question about greatness in the kingdom indicates that they viewed themselves as its princes. By outlining for them this pattern of church discipline, Jesus deflated any notion they might have entertained of becoming the princes of the churches. Jesus swept them all aside as potential authority figures, along with any prelate, cleric, pastor, bishop, elder, or deacon who might claim ownership of the church. He placed the authority to administer the church and to make the decisions that shape its life and affect its constituency squarely on the congregation. In a community of servants, nobody may swagger as its big boss and nobody may parade bejeweled humility as a claim for preeminence and power.

This form of governance represented such a radical departure from everything the disciples had ever known that Jesus immediately provided two explanations to support his teaching. The first was that heaven approves church decisions that are made corporately (Matt. 18:18). The book of Acts provides some insight about this teaching. The decisions made by a local congregation are also identified as decisions made by the Holy Spirit (Acts 13:3–4; 15:22–23, 28). The rationale for this view is probably that the Spirit, who indwells all believers, eventually speaks with one collective voice when the members of a congregation are attuned to the Spirit and to each other.

The second reason given by Christ for his teaching on corporate decision-making is closely related to the previous one. The Lord is always present in the midst of a worshiping community gathered in his name (Matt. 18:19–20). Because of his presence, two or three heads bowed together have a better chance of coming up with the mind of Christ than one dominant individual making decisions for the rest of them.

Later developments in the life of the church reveal that the apostles took this teaching to heart and obeyed it. When a contention arose within the church of Jerusalem, the Twelve gathered the whole congregation and submitted a proposal to "the whole group," which was accepted and implemented by the congregation (Acts 6:1–6). The apostles had well retained their Master's teaching. They facilitated the process and got out of the way for the congregation to act.

Later, when an even more serious dispute arose among the churches concerning the inclusion of believing Gentiles into the body, the decisions were not imposed hierarchically but were made corporately by the churches involved (15:1–31). The church at Antioch sent delegates to the church in Jerusalem in order to resolve the problem (vv. 3–4). The final decision was rendered by "the apostles and elders, with the whole church" (v. 22). It was then sent to Antioch and submitted to the congregation gathered together (v. 30). The apostles did not make the decisions for the congregations but involved them in the process during each phase of its progress.

In Corinth, two Christians from the same congregation were apparently embroiled in a lawsuit against each other (1 Cor. 6:1–8). In addressing this scandalous situation, the apostle Paul carefully refrained from asking any authority figure to intervene, and he himself refused to hand down a decision to settle the matter. Instead, he called upon the two parties to resolve the problem on their own by accepting to be wronged or even cheated instead of fighting each other (v. 7). As an alternative option, he called upon the congregation to produce somebody "wise enough to judge a dispute between believers" (v. 5). Again, the church was expected to take care of its affairs without authoritarian interference from ecclesiastical office holders.

The Philippian church was disrupted by a contention between two of its members (Phil. 4:2–3). There were appointed overseers and deacons available to the congregation (1:1), but Paul did not call on them to referee the dispute. Instead, he pleaded with the two leaders to reconcile, and he requested another member of the congregation to help them do so. The overseers and the deacons were apparently kept out of the process to allow it to unfold and take care of the problem on its own.

In other words, the apostles took seriously their Master's teaching about the governance system that he had assigned for the churches. Except for the Pastoral Letters, leaders are never presented in the New Testament as imposing decisions to congregations. They either encouraged congregations to come up with their own decisions, or they worked in concert with congregations to help them make the right decisions.

This kind of coordinated action took place in the case of the incestuous man who was scandalously tolerated as a church member in Corinth. The apostle Paul laid out the principles that were relevant to the case and asked the church to assemble together so that the whole congregation could participate in taking the appropriate action (1 Cor. 5:3–5). Because the church is a community of servants, all members are at the same time empowered and mutually submitted. The church is the community where all "submit to one another out of reverence for Christ" (Eph. 5:21).

Of course, Jesus' model of the church as a community of servants raises a host of questions as to the function of leadership and the use of authority within the new community. Since the New Testament reports the appointment of leaders such as elders in all churches, their roles must be defined, not in terms of current ecclesiastical traditions (which vary with time and place and with denominational polities), but according to the teachings of the New Testament. In the following analysis, three such functions are identified as the main responsibilities of church leaders. They are the spiritual watchcare and nurture of the church, the equipping of the laity for ministry, and the ministry of intervention in situations of crisis.

3. Spiritual Watchcare

The spiritual well-being of the church is of concern to every member of the congregation, but responsibility for its maintenance devolves more particularly on the leaders of the local church. They must watch over the spiritual health of the congregation with the same attention they give to the nurture of their own spiritual lives (Acts 20:28). Their oversight is of the same nature as the watchcare of shepherds with their flocks: "The good shepherd lays down his life for the sheep" (John

10:11). Likewise, good church leaders do not take care of the flock because they are "greedy for money" but because they are "eager to serve" (1 Peter 5:2). Like the work of good servants, their ministry is self-sacrificial. However, should leaders ever imagine that the church belongs to them instead of seeing themselves merely as its servants, they are strongly reminded that it is exclusively "the church of God, which he bought with his own blood" (Acts 20:28).

It is Christ who provides the church with such servant leaders by gifting "some to be apostles, some to be prophets, some to be evangelists, and some to be pastors and teachers" (Eph. 4:11). Because their task is that of watchcare and shepherding, it is often called "pastoral care," a term derived from the Latin word *pastor*, meaning "shepherd." The overall purpose of such gifts and ministries is to speak to people "for their strengthening, encouragement and comfort" (1 Cor. 14:3).

Although providing pastoral care is the main responsibility of those leaders, they do not have an exclusive monopoly on it. People in the congregation must also be competent to fulfill the same ministries. The apostle Paul expected church members to be "complete in knowledge and competent to instruct one another" (Rom. 15:14), to "teach and admonish one another with all wisdom" (Col. 3:16), and to "encourage one another and build each other up" (1 Thess. 5:11). Amazingly, these very same terms Paul used to describe this ministry of congregations watching over themselves and caring for their own growth, he also used to describe his own ministry as an apostle: "We proclaim [Christ], admonishing and teaching everyone with all wisdom, so that we may present everyone perfect in Christ" (Col. 1:28). Paul expanded the responsibilities of pastoral care so that it became congregational self-care.

The reason for this blurring of the lines between the responsibilities of leaders and laity is that the church is a community of servants who join together in full partnership to achieve their goals. Getting the job done is more important than trying to determine who belongs where in a structure of hierarchy. The church is where people can minister side by side as team members without having to worry about considerations of rank and position, as they do in the military.

There is no doubt that the military could not function without hierarchy. But the church can function the way it does because its members are guided by the same indwelling Holy Spirit—a claim that can hardly be made for the military. Church members work together as a community of servants. Within this arrangement, the distinctive responsibility of leaders, who might be tempted to view themselves as being "great" or "first," is to act as "servant" and "slave" to the others (Matt. 20:26–27). In so doing, they act as "examples to the flock" (1 Peter 5:3).

Since the task of the church will never be completed until the End, ministry may never become static. The gospel is a dynamic force, whose field of application never runs short of challenges. Whenever a church goes into a maintenance mode because the congregation and the leaders think they have arrived, it becomes bureaucratic and institutional. Slow death is the result. Where there is no vision, the people perish. One important aspect of the leaders' watchcare for the church is to formulate its corporate vision for and with the congregation, and to interpret it into a clear statement of mission that can be detailed in periodically updated strategic planning sessions. Such an approach provides incentive for the progress of the work of the gospel and helps preserve the integrity of its focus.

When leaders try to impose their vision on the congregation, it remains their own. Vision must be developed in concert with others and shared in ways that elicit ownership and create motivation for its accomplishment. The New Testament is replete with examples of such visionary servant leadership. At a time, for example, when the church at Jerusalem was comfortably ensconced in the shadow of the temple (Acts 5:42), Stephen and his diaspora companions saw a need for the church to make a clean break with Judaism (7:48–53). The conservative-minded Jewish Christians of Jerusalem were satisfied with maintaining the status quo, an uneasy stalemate of mutual tolerance that had emerged from earlier confrontations between the newborn church and official Judaism. However, the progressive-minded dissenters were obedient to Christ's vision of a church that would not stand still until kingdom came. This vision-casting cost Stephen his life, but under its impact, the church started to move again and to fulfill the Great Commission (8:1, 4; 11:19). Others took on Stephen's challenge and started preaching the gospel to the Gentiles (11:20–21). As a result, the Gentile church was launched, and the apostle Paul was recruited as its chief visionary promoter (vv. 25–26; 13:1–2). The rest became history.

4. Equipping for Ministry

Another responsibility of leaders is to equip God's people to do ministry (Eph. 4:11–13). The biblical job description of church leaders is not to take it upon themselves to do the ministry of the church but to encourage the congregation to do it by training "God's people for works of service, so that the body of Christ may be built up." The specific purpose of this equipping ministry concerns the growth and the expansion of the local church, the building up of the body of Christ. This task is so formidable that it lies beyond the capacity of any leader or group of leaders to achieve it by themselves. They must mobilize all the human and spiritual resources available in their community.

The highest attainment achievable by leaders is to reproduce their expertise in "ordinary" people and to turn them into leaders. This is also the best expression of servanthood: leaders who train others to excel beyond them. What John the Baptist said of Jesus could well be the motto of servant leaders with regard to their charges: "He must become greater, I must become less" (John 3:30). Servant leadership is to empower others to become greater than oneself.

The biblically prescribed mechanism to equip the body for ministry is the discovery and the utilization of spiritual gifts. Heavy, authoritarian, self-promoting leadership smothers lay initiative and stifles the use of such gifts. It parades its own stuff and derides inexperience. Servant leadership, on the other hand, is like the work of a patient coach, who discovers the potential talents of team members and enables them to take the field while cheering for them from the sidelines.

The best contribution leaders can make is to train others to become leaders in their own areas of expertise by helping them to discover their spiritual gifts and by showing them how to actualize their newfound skills in the work of the kingdom. In the community of servants, ministry is not leader-centered but congregation-based. The congregation is not there to support leaders to do ministry. It's the other way around: The leaders are there to support the congregation to do ministry.

There is no other area of the life of the church for which this principle of servant leadership is more crucial to church growth than its application to the evangelistic outreach of the church. There were "evangelists" in the early church. But their function is described as preparing "God's people for works of service, so that the body of Christ may be built up" (Eph. 4:11–12). Indeed, the people best qualified to carry out the evangelistic mandate of the church are not professional evangelists or those occupying pulpits. As Billy Graham put it in 1995, "Evangelism is not just a crowd of people. Evangelism is more effective when we are able to do it on a personal basis." By a strange reversion, the greater the focus on pulpit evangelism, altar calls, evangelistic crusades, revivals, and special meeting, the less incentive remains for lay people to become personally involved in witnessing for their faith. They are made to feel that a better qualified professional can do it in their place.

But let evangelists and pastors train every believer to be a witness, they will be able to watch the outreach of the church become multiplied exponentially. Lay believers are the best qualified people to reach the unchurched. They interact with them day in and day out in the natural settings of family, neighborhoods, work, school, and leisure. They speak the same language and are in touch with the real world within which their unchurched friends and relatives move and live. They can go and establish an authentic witness in places where no evangelist could ever penetrate, much less get a hearing.

Unfortunately, what often passes for personal evangelism is the transposition of the methods of mass evangelism to the level of interpersonal encounters. Too many lay evangelists are being trained to quick-draw unbelievers with a barrage of Bible verses or spiritual laws in order to bring them to an immediate decision for Christ. But eventually, they either feel unqualified to grandstand as a miniature, pulpit-pounding professional evangelist, or they meet with enough failure and justified rebuffs to become discouraged from ever trying again.

The Scriptures suggest an approach that is accessible to every believer, even to those who do not have the gift of evangelism. It consists of establishing relationships of authentic, disinterested, and nonmanipulative friendship with potential seekers and simply allowing the Holy Spirit to use the association in his own time and in his own way as a vehicle for Christian witness. Thus, after Levi the tax collector became a follower of Jesus, he invited his colleagues and his friends to a party where they had opportunity to meet Jesus (Luke 5:27–29). Likewise, Andrew and Philip became acquainted with Jesus and shared their newfound faith with others in the context of the natural settings of family and friendship relations (John 1:40–49).

In order to be credible, this grassroots relational evangelism must be modeled by church leaders, pastors, and professional evangelists. As difficult as it may be for such people to establish authentic relations of friendship with unbelievers, they must learn to befriend potential seekers whom they would normally ignore. No amount of exhortation can motivate lay people to do the right thing as the example of pastors who practice what they preach.

When modern Christians act more like Jesus, who was a friend of sinners, and less like the Pharisees, who took pride in their righteous separation from sinners, they can share their witness in congenial settings instead of inflicting it where it is not wanted. The right to witness must be earned. It may not be arrogantly assumed without incurring the rejection of the gospel.

One may not rightfully speak of the love of Christ to a seeker without becoming its incarnation. Servant evangelism enables people who think of themselves as ordinary to enter the wonderful world of interrelationships and to use it for God, who is himself a relational being.

Concurrently and in true servant form, the local church should make available a periodic and carefully crafted seeker event that is appropriately customized to be intelligible to interested unbelievers, so as to expose them to the life of Christian community and to awaken them to the realization of their need for the gospel. As a result, conversions to Christ and transformed lives become predictable and recurring realities. Seekers become believers, they are integrated in the life of the church, and, in turn, they act as servant messengers with their acquaintances, relatives, friends, coworkers, and neighbors. Such an abundance of literature is available on the "seeker" approach to congregation-based evangelism that describing it here in detail is superfluous.

However, a caution must be sounded for churches that engage in seeker outreach prematurely. Trying to contextualize a traditional worship service by giving it a contemporary face-lift with "drums and drama" will uselessly alienate a segment of the congregation and fail to attract seekers. Except for pioneer missionary efforts, biblically defined evangelism is always congregation-based. It presupposes a congregation comprised of dedicated and servant-minded laypeople, who have intentionally become a cohesive and highly motivated community complete with small groups and ministry teams. Only then, when structures for the integration of new converts are in place and when the vision for the expansion of community becomes a driving passion for the whole group, is it advisable to launch seeker events and to encourage members of the congregation to bring their friends. Initiating a seeker program without the backing of a committed community will condemn it to failure.

The church functions optimally when ministry is a universally shared privilege rather than the burden of a few professionals.

The apostle Peter described the interconnectedness of ministries in the local church with these words: "Like good stewards of the manifold grace of God, serve one another with whatever gift each of you has received" (1 Peter 4:10 NRSV). In the community of servants, both leaders and laity must be bent on serving one another with whatever gifts each has received in order to accomplish their shared task. Within this perspective, the distinction between leaders and laity has significance only inasmuch as it facilitates the fulfillment of the corporate mission.

5. Church Discipline

The third area of special responsibility incumbent on servant leaders is their ministry of intervention for the purpose of preventing crises or resolving them should they occur. Under normal circumstances, there is no need for leaders to intervene forcefully or to exercise authority as they watch over the life of the church. As a matter of fact, a heavy-handed approach to spiritual watchcare and to ministry development can only be counterproductive. Positive results are better obtained from a servant posture that elicits emulation rather than from assertions of authority or the use of coercion.

However, because the church is not immune to infiltrations of sin, error, and dissension, leaders gifted with discernment must be on the alert to defuse potentially harmful situations and to deal decisively with trouble when it develops. From supportive servants under normal circumstances, leaders must assume the role of wise judges in situations of crisis (1 Cor. 6:5). Such disciplinary interventions are described in the New Testament as a two-step procedure. In a first phase, the offender must be warned once, and then a second time should the first intervention remain unfruitful (Titus 3:10–11). The second phase requires the severance of unrepentant individuals (v. 10; cf. 2 Thess. 3:14–15). However, disciplinary action is not punitive or vengeful. Rather, it is intended to protect the church from harmful influences and to bring persons under discipline to repentance and to eventual restoration (2 Thess. 3:15).

When the apostle Paul foresaw some of the troubles that would befall the church at Ephesus, he warned the elders of the church of impending disasters and told them, "Be on your guard" (Acts 20:31). Unfortunately, the vigilance of the Ephesian elders did not suffice to forestall attacks on the congregation. As surveyed above, the Pastoral Letters reflect situations of advanced deterioration. Consequently, Paul ordered the religious equivalent of martial law with extraordinary reinforcements of existing authority structures and severe restrictions on access to ministry. In other words, the exercise of authority within the local church is a legitimate function of leadership but mainly for preventative and remedial reasons, as a safety net in cases of emergency. Otherwise, there are no instructions in the New Testament for leaders to minister from a position other than that of servant.

The polarity between the exercise of authority and servant ministry is grounded in the teaching of Jesus (Matt. 20:25–28). The apostle Paul did not teach differently. He could adopt either an authority figure approach or a servant attitude in his relations with the churches he had established. He tried to call to reason some "arrogant people" who were troubling the Corinthian church. With a prospective visit to their city in view, he offered the alternative of going to them "with a whip, or in love and with a gentle spirit" (1 Cor. 4:21). No doubt, Paul would have preferred to go to Corinth as a loving servant. But if necessary, according to the safety net principle, he would not have hesitated to exercise his apostolic authority and to appear on the scene as a stern disciplinarian.

As reluctant as Paul was to use authority in his dealings with the churches, he was ready to do so, even to the point of being "harsh," should the need have required it (2 Cor. 13:10). This appeal to authority for cases of exception indicates that relations of authority cannot be accepted as the modus operandi or as the normative way of doing church work under usual circumstances. Recourse to authority is reserved, according to the New Testament, for intervention in sinful or deleterious situations that require corrective action (v. 2).

Since leaders are accountable for their ministry of watchcare, they are obligated to take their task seriously. The appropriate response of congregations to justified authority interventions is obedience and submission (Heb. 13:17). Otherwise, the unresolved troubles that require the strong intervention of leaders would cause their ministry to be "a burden" instead of a source of joy. Moreover, the ministry of the leaders "would be of no advantage" to disobedient and unsubmissive church members since the risk of being "carried away by all kinds of strange teachings" would persist (v. 9). God's gift of accountable leadership is wasted on the disorderly who persist in their rebellion (6:4–8).

If congregations can persist in their disobedience and resist justified authority interventions, the opposite may also happen. Leaders may abuse congregations and exercise authority without justification. The apostle Paul recognized that the authority entrusted to leaders by the Lord to build up could also be used destructively to pull down (2 Cor. 10:8) and to tear down (13:10). For this very reason, the apostle Peter warned church leaders not to lord it over those who are entrusted to them (1 Peter 5:3). Originally, this was the reason for the Lord's categorical rejection of authority as a normative mode for structuring community governance when he forbade his followers to be "rulers," to "lord it over," and "to exercise authority" among themselves (Matt. 20:25–28).

The disorders that affected the Ephesian church provide an instance of authority abuse by the women who were forbidden to teach in 1 Timothy 2. Paul reveals that some were unstable, double-minded in their allegiances, "always learning but never able to acknowledge the truth" (2 Tim. 3:6–7). They had been caught disseminating falsehood "from house to house," and they had "turned away to follow Satan" (1 Tim. 5:13, 15). Paul ordered the Ephesian women not to teach because that was precisely what they had been doing; they had been teaching falsehood.

What makes the Ephesian prohibition intriguing is that, in the parallel letter of Titus, Paul took exactly the opposite position in regard to women teaching. He encouraged some women in the churches of Crete to teach. In fact, he specifically enjoined them "to teach what is good" (Titus 2:3), despite the fact that there were male elders appointed in every church who were qualified to teach "sound doctrine and refute those who oppose it" (1:5, 9). Paul directed the women to be "teachers of what is good" without placing restrictions on the age or gender of those who should be taught by them, except that their teaching ministry should include younger women who needed their mature wisdom (2:4).

It was probably in reaction to the negative experience with the Ephesian female teachers that Paul insisted for the Cretan women to be teachers "of what is good." Obviously, Paul felt much more secure with the Cretan women teaching than with their counterparts doing so in Ephesus. This may indicate how heavily the pagan legacy of the city of Ephesus had weighed on its women. Because the religious life of the city was dominated by the worship of the great goddess, women held significant positions in the pagan ritual of the local temple. When some of the same women joined the church, it may have been only too easy for them to bring along some of their pagan habits into Christian worship.

The false teaching that the Ephesian women were spreading from home to home was reason enough to suspend them from the teaching function, but, according to the biblical text, there may also have been baggage imported from pagan rituals. It had to do with the arrogance and the impetuousness that accompanied the false teaching. It appears that the trouble-prone Ephesian women were so obnoxious that Paul had to temper their abusive ways by telling them to "learn in quietness and full submission" and to "be silent" (1 Tim. 2:11–12). The women's misbehavior is not specified, but it is reflected in the reference to "authority" in Paul's command for them "not to teach or to have authority over a man" (v. 12).

The prohibition for either men or women to exercise authority over anyone else within the Christian community was nothing new. It was a universal rule that normally applied to all Christians because it was grounded in the teaching of Jesus (Matt.

20:25–26). Obviously, Paul's prohibition was aimed at something that the Ephesian women were doing in defiance of this universal rule.

The wording of this prohibition in 1 Timothy 2:12 presents a revealing feature. When Paul forbade women to have "authority" over men, he avoided using the usual New Testament word for "authority." Instead, he chose a rare word, found only here in the New Testament. The problem with this rare word is that its precise meaning is unclear. Since there is no other occurrence of it in the New Testament, its usage cannot be verified with the help of other control texts. However, there is an opinion among biblical scholars that it refers in a general way to the excessive use of authority and, perhaps even more specifically, to the abusive manner with which authority may be assumed. In any case, the lexical evidence suggests that the Ephesian women were doing something bad in terms of authority abuse that no one else was doing within the Christian community.

The excesses that caused the Ephesian women's temporary removal from the teaching ministry illustrate how easily the use of authority can be turned into abuse. Such abuse occurs readily when hierarchical structures are allowed to replace networks of servanthood as the infrastructure of community, and when recourse to authority becomes the norm in Christian relations instead of being held in reserve as a remedial resource, to be utilized mainly for cases of emergency and prevention.

The church's obedience to Scriptures for the fulfillment of its mission is at stake. Hierarchical structures are ponderous, stifling, and sterile. Flattening them into interconnected small groups and ministry teams holds the only hope for local churches to release the irresistible dynamic of servanthood, and to turn dead or dying institutions into invincible communities of oneness that will devour the world.

B. LEADERSHIP AND SPIRITUAL GIFTS

The Pastoral Letters contain the most elaborate specifications found in the New Testament for appointive leadership functions, but they make hardly any mention of the spiritual gifts that normally justify and undergird such ministries. Spiritual gifts seem to have been replaced by requirements of status and experience derived from managing cohesive families. As noted above, this peculiarity resulted from the exceptionally difficult circumstances of the churches to which the Pastorals were addressed. Otherwise, New Testament norms require that the performance of all ministries be dependent on the gifts made available to local congregations by the Holy Spirit. Consequently, not less than for other church ministries, leadership assignments are expected to be gift-specific.

It is abundantly clear in the New Testament that, in granting his gifts, the Holy Spirit distributes them equitably so that the ministries of the church are appropriately portioned out to all the members of the body, and that no one individual is burdened with responsibility for all the ministries simultaneously. The specificity of the various spiritual gifts requires that they be allotted to different individuals according to the grace granted to each believer (Rom. 12:6–8). To each is given the manifestation of the Spirit so that each member of the body may have a distinct ministry (1 Cor. 12:8–11) and so that not all should minister in the same gift area (vv. 28–30).

Scripture makes it clear that this gift-specific diversification of ministries is indispensable for the proper functioning of the body. It is especially important that the leadership or "equipping" ministries of the church be kept distinct from each other so that their functions can be effectively performed (Eph. 4:11). Those ministries are never lumped together in Scripture as if one individual were supposed to cover them all. This does not mean that a person cannot be multi-gifted so as to be able to perform in more than one ministry area or to equip others to do ministry in more than one area. But the doctrine of the diversification of spiritual gifts means that no one individual can ever receive all the gifts and thus wear all the leadership hats and perform all the ministries single-handedly. Such a model of centralized ministry is not only absent in the New Testament but is also forbidden by it (1 Cor. 12:20–21).

This is the issue on which clear scriptural directives and widely accepted ecclesiastical traditions collide head-on. Amazingly, tradition wins out over Scripture. The change from congregation-based ministries to the emergence of the "minister" as the performer of ministry for the local church did not occur overnight. It was the result of a long, historical process that began in postapostolic times, reached its full development in the medieval church, and was left essentially unchallenged by the Protestant Reformation.

This gradual replacement of the priesthood of all believers by the ministry of a professional clergy has had disastrous consequences in two areas. The first is the disfranchisement of the laity from ministry. Awed by the elitist image projected by trained specialists, the average church member shrinks away from ministry involvements or reduces them to marginally supportive roles.

The other deleterious aspect of the priestly model of ministry is the devastating effect it has on the ministers themselves. The clergy-dominant system of doing church places on pastors the unrealistic burden of acting as if they were universally gifted so as to be able to carry successfully the multitude of responsibilities that constitute the life of local congregations. Because no individual can claim to possess all the spiritual gifts necessary to fulfill the complex demands of ministry, such pastors often feel obligated to minister outside of their gift areas. As a result, they are in a no-win situation. Ministry easily becomes an incinerator for candidates to burn out. No minister, however gifted, can do everything, be everywhere, and meet all the expectations that are tacitly or explicitly built into a pastor's job description. Biblically defined, the ministry of a local body requires the mobilization of its constituency. Congregations that foist their own responsibilities on their minister lock that person into a situation of despair.

Ordination

To make things worse, this manner of doing church has become institutionalized and given an aura of sanctity with the practice of "ordination." At best, ordination is a public recognition of the calling of a candidate to ministry. At worst, it is a sacramental ritual that is thought to confer some spiritual grace on the candidate to habilitate and set him apart for a ministry to which laypeople are not supposed to qualify. In either case, the practice has scant biblical support, but it is heavy with traditional accretions that vary from denomination to denomination.

It is commonly assumed that a connection exists between ordination and the ceremony of the laying on of hands, as if the latter justified the former. Although there are several reports of laying on of hands in the New Testament record, none can be understood as having much to do with ordination as it is currently practiced. Jesus laid hands on children and on the sick (Mark 6:5; 10:13–16; Luke 13:13; etc.), but he is never reported to have done so for the disciples or for anyone he commissioned to Christian service.

The apostles laid hands on the Seven to appoint them to "wait on tables" so that they could devote themselves "to prayer and the ministry of the word" (Acts 6:2–6). Ironically, those who receive ordination today are not the ones who "wait on the tables," but those who perform the "ministry of the word."

The laying of hands on Barnabas and Saul for the specific purpose of sending them on their missionary journey is often adduced in support of the ritual of ordination (Acts 13:2–3). However, since both Barnabas and Saul had already been recognized by the church as functioning "prophets and teachers" prior to receiving the laying on of hands, it is impossible to view this instance as a case of ordination to ministry (v. 1). Twice, the apostles laid hands on new converts as a sign of their reception of the Holy Spirit, but those instances had nothing to do with the ordination of selected individuals to ministry (8:17–18; 19:6).

The apostle Paul reveals that Timothy had a spiritual gift (*charisma*) that was given to him "through a prophetic message when the body of elders laid their hands" on him (1 Tim. 4:14). This instance can hardly be identified as a case of ordination since it was the occasion for the impartation of a gift rather than the recognition of the ministry that had resulted from that gift—namely, the ability to teach and preach (v. 13).

The charismatic function of the laying on of hands was confirmed in Paul's own experience when he laid his hands on Timothy to impart to him "the gift of God" (2 Tim. 1:6), which, according to the immediate context, seems to have been a gift for bold witness (vv. 7–8). Again, this instance cannot be interpreted as a case of ordination since it was the impartation of a gift rather than its recognition and confirmation in an ordination ceremony. In any case, "ordination" is never mentioned in the New Testament, and much less listed as a "gift." Therefore, the "gift" that Timothy was expected to "fan into flame" (v. 6 NIV) or "rekindle" (RSV) had nothing to do with any alleged ordination. These two instances were more akin to those in Acts 8 and 19, where the laying on of hands was a sign of common identity in the sharing of the blessing and ministry of the Holy Spirit.

Paul gave a command to Timothy that is sometimes adduced as supportive evidence for the ritual of ordination. He wrote to the younger man not to "be hasty in the laying on of hands" and not to "share in the sins of others" (1 Tim. 5:22). But what was forbidden in this statement can hardly qualify as ordination to ministry. That action was a personal initiative on the part of Timothy, which he might perform prematurely and for which he then had to assume responsibility in case of misjudgment. A personal initiative such as suggested in this passage is not compatible with the practice of ordination to ministry, which calls for public recognition and affirmation.

Moreover, the identity of the candidates for Timothy's laying on of hands is open to question. It is unlikely that Paul's caution is aimed at the "ordination" of bishop/overseers and deacons in Ephesus since the rigid criteria for their selection excluded the possibility of hasty appointments or of sinful behavior on their part (3:1–13). Paul's statement was probably intended to discourage Timothy from recognizing and affirming the spiritual gifts of members of the congregation before he could ascertain the quality of their character and their spiritual walk. This would

have been consistent with Paul's policy of temporary retrenchment of ministry in Ephesus. In either case, a rite of laying on
of hands that could be initiated individually, hastily, injudiciously,
and with a number of people from the same congregation can
hardly be invoked to support a doctrine for the ordination of
clergy as it is practiced today.

The meaning of this reference to the laying on of hands is
probably consistent with that of the other two references found
in the Pastorals (1 Tim. 4:14; 2 Tim. 1:6). Rather than signifying
the induction of individuals into a special category of "ministers,"
the laying on of hands seems to have been used on people who
were already doing ministry as a repeatable sign of encouragement to them for tackling specific challenges with the fullness of
the Spirit. Such an explanation would be consistent with the laying of hands on the Seven (Acts 6) and on Barnabas and Saul
(Acts 13). As such, the laying on of hands would not signify
induction into the ministry but commissioning for specific assignments, some as seemingly menial as serving at tables.

Such an understanding would also provide an explanation for the
otherwise perplexing linkage in the letter to the Hebrews of basic
instructions about baptism (as induction of new believers into the
community) with instructions about the laying on of hands (as
induction of *all* baptized believers into ministry, Heb. 6:2).

The importance of the doctrine of spiritual gifts for the communal life of the church can easily be ignored (1 Cor. 12:1).
Because of renewed sensitivity to the reality of spiritual gifts,
many thoughtful Christians are reconsidering the meaning of
ordination and the assumptions that underlie the way it has been
traditionally practiced. Such persons are strongly urged to check
a book that was already recommended above: Greg Ogden's *The
New Reformation: Returning the Ministry to the People of God*
(Zondervan, 1992). This section on leadership and spiritual gifts
assumes the availability of this excellent book as a source of reliable guidance for every churchgoer concerned about the biblical definitions of ministry, leadership, and ordination.

From this perspective, appointive leadership offices are nothing more than the exercise of spiritual gifts recognized and affirmed by a local congregation. Many church groups define the recognition of such offices as "ordination." Neither the term nor the concept is biblical if it glorifies and elevates some ministries within the church above others. Since all spiritual gifts are distributed by the Spirit, all believers are "ordained" by God into ministry.

Although the impact of the different gift-derived ministries on the overall work of the church may vary, the worth of the persons and of the gifts is the same before God (1 Cor. 12:22–25). It should be the same for the community. At times, it may be appropriate to recognize formally a gift and encourage the ministry that derives from it through a ritual such as the laying on of hands. But never should such a recognition result in a stratification of ministries that would produce what Ogden calls a "split-level" congregation and destroy the oneness of the community.

The call to ministry is every Christian's passionate response at the intersection of community-affirmed giftedness and of needs crying for intervention. Consequently, every Christian who discovers his or her spiritual gift and is affirmed in it by one's local congregation is, by that very fact, ordained by God to do ministry. In the light of the limited data available in the New Testament for the formulation of a theology of ordination, such a practice should be viewed as having traditional relevance rather than biblical sanction.

In other words, to prevent any believer in good standing within the community from using fully his or her spiritual gift because of restrictions that pertain to "ordination" is to allow church traditions to take precedence over biblical imperatives. According to Scriptures, spiritual gifts constitute the basis for ministry. Because they are all God-ordained, they must be treated with respect and solicitude by the community rather than with petty discriminations and exclusions (Rom. 12:4–8; 1 Cor. 12:14–25; 1 Peter 4:10–11). Church leaders would be better inspired to exhort all believers to use their gifts optimally for the kingdom rather than argue with them about what they cannot do in God's service.

The cohesive power that unites the various gifts and ministries of a congregation and causes them to function harmoniously as one body is nothing less than the total involvement of the Godhead in the work of the local church: the Spirit in relation to the different gifts, the Lord Christ in relation to the different kinds of service, and God the Father in relation to the different kinds of working (1 Cor. 12:4–6). The distribution of the gifts and ministries is the sovereign privilege of the Spirit (v. 11); but God is the one who arranges them in relation to each other just as he wants them to be (vv. 18, 24b), so that the harmonious whole constitutes the body of Christ (v. 27). From cooperative oneness above proceeds functional oneness within the human community. The imposition of humanly derived, split-level dichotomies on this divinely ordered oneness can only defeat the purposes they are intended to achieve.

At the human level, oneness does not just happen on its own. It takes hard work to bring it about, and once it is there, it takes hard work to protect it. A fallen world dominated by rulership applies relentless pressure on the church to stratify its relationships into hierarchy. The deceptive point of access of hierarchy into the Christian community is through leadership roles misconstrued as positions of power. Not confusing gifts of leadership with positions of power would go a long way toward the protection of community. The following is a random listing of some suggestions for clergy and laity to work together for the decentralization of church ministries:

- Train laypeople to develop their spiritual gifts and invest them in ministry teams.
- Train church staff not to do themselves what laypeople can do but to help them do it.
- Allow leadership and ministry teams to have one or two retreats every year.
- Train church leadership to maintain a low servant profile.
- Always think of leadership in terms of team leadership.

- Elect church officers in consideration of the spiritual gifts needed on the board(s) of the church.
- Elect church officers for one-year renewable terms. This allows for flexibility should changes be necessary and for continuity in the case of proven spiritual gifts.
- The "senior" pastor should be a board member, equally accountable to it and not its chair.
- Select and appoint pastors in function of the spiritual gifts required by the church for its next stage of development.
- Do not expect pastors to minister outside of their gift areas.
- As soon as the growth of the church justifies it, appoint multiple staff with complementary gifting.
- Expect the staff to work as a team, even to team-teach and to team-preach.
- Expect each leader to mentor individually his or her potential replacement.
- Keep communication lines open between congregation and leadership through periodic newsletters and congregational Question and Answer sessions.
- To defuse potential conflicts, require that complaints and grievances be submitted to the church board.
- Do not dismiss a staff or office-holder without requiring the person involved to explain to the congregation the reason for his or her departure.
- Never allow style of leadership to devalue persons in need of leadership.
- Train staff, lay leaders, and congregation always to think of themselves as servants, servants, servants (1 Cor. 3:5; 4:1).

C. PLURAL LEADERSHIP

The simplistic premises that underlie authority-based leadership enable dominant individuals to establish themselves as rulers because their task is relatively uncomplicated. Right or wrong, they make the decisions. They are not required to submit to the painstaking process of negotiation and deliberation. If they do, they still control final outcomes. Might makes right.

Not so with leadership biblically defined. Because of the exacting complexities of servant leadership, no one individual can presume to assume all the responsibilities that it entails. In a hierarchical system, the strong man or the person in charge hands down decisions that may not be questioned or criticized. Even if issues are allowed to be discussed, the strong individual leader arrogates the right to make final decisions for the group. The servant leadership approach is much more subtle and therefore much more demanding.

A typical approach may require servant leaders to bring to the attention of the community matters of concern that affect its life so that the group may, in turn, commission them to seek resolutions (Acts 15:2–3). This may require groups of people to meet in order to consider such matters together (vv. 4, 6). Their consultation may involve much discussion (v. 7) and even times when the whole assembly becomes silent (v. 12). Opportunity must be given to all competent people to participate in the discussion (vv. 12–13) until a consensus is reached (v. 22); this then becomes the decision of the Holy Spirit (v. 28), because the community was involved together in discerning the mind of God. Servant leadership operates on the basis of group consensus or of representative consensus, not of unilateral, autocratic, top-down decision-making.

The New Testament contains a strong rationale for the necessity of authority structures in secular society (Matt. 22:16–21; Rom. 13:1–7; 1 Tim. 2:1–2; Titus 3:1; 1 Peter 2:13–17). Because the fallen world does not have the mind of Christ, it cannot function in an orderly fashion without someone taking charge and enforcing rules.

A similar apologetic for the practice of authority within the church cannot be found in the New Testament. If anything, the Scriptures explicitly forbid Christians to run their communities in the manner of "the rulers of the Gentiles" or of "their high officials [who] exercise authority over them" (Matt. 20:25). The secular world is governed by ruler-to-subject relations. The distinctive mark of relations in Christian communities, however, is that they conform to a subject-to-subject model of interactive life (Eph. 5:21). The world cannot function effectively without leaders controlling their subjects; the church cannot function effectively when leaders control their constituency.

The Holy Spirit's dynamic for community is not for some to control others but for all to be mutually submissive as servants. In this perspective, the task of Christian leaders is not to use positions of authority to control the community but to band together as servant leaders to work for the best interests of the community. There may be times when control may be necessary to correct evil behavior, thus serving the best interests of the group, but only as measures of exception in situations of crisis and never as a normal way of life.

Under normal circumstances, the purpose of leadership is to enable the group to exercise its own corporate responsibility. Because of checks and balances, a group of leaders is less likely to become corrupted and to usurp the authority of the community than a strong individual leader who might gain ascendancy over it. When it comes to leadership, there is safety in numbers.

The pressure exerted on the Christian mind to conform to the pattern of this world and to impose on Christian communities orders of hierarchy extraneous to it is relentless (2 Cor. 11:20; Gal. 4:8–9; 5:1). The power of such influences is demonstrated by the proliferation of religious sects that claim scriptural support to subject their converts to authoritarian and controlling designs. It can even affect the translations of the Scriptures we hold in our hands, as with unwarranted insertions of the word "authority" where it is absent in the original text (Heb. 13:17 NIV; 1 Peter 3:1; 5:5 NRSV). The best defense against autocratic takeovers of Christian congregations is a constitutionally protected plurality of leaders. Such a form of governance is also the church's best demonstration to the secular world of the purity of its designs and a clear witness of its distinctiveness as authentic Christian community.

There is no evidence in the New Testament that any early Christian community existed that was under the local leadership of one dominant individual. In fact, there is no precedent and no legitimization in the Bible for the one-pastor church model. All the appointive functions mentioned in the New Testament in connection with the leadership of local churches are consistently in the plural number. For instance, not all churches had bishops or overseers, but those who did had not one but several. The leaders of the Ephesian church were told that the Holy Spirit had made them "overseers" of the flock (Acts 20:28). When writing to the church at Philippi, Paul greeted the congregation and, separately, the "overseers" (Phil. 1:1). When he wrote to Titus, Paul directed the appointment of elders, whom he also identified with the functions of "overseer" (Titus 1:5–7). Leadership, as defined in the New Testament, is always plural.

Despite the fact that the apostles stayed in the Jerusalem church for a time, acting as its first leaders, they shared the leadership of the congregation with a group of elders (Acts 15:4, 6, 22), who remained long after the apostles were gone (21:18). Elders are not mentioned in connection with every church. But when they are, the reference is always to a plurality of elders and never to one lone leader. Whether they are designated as a "body of elders" (1 Tim. 4:14) or simply as "elders," this form of leadership was always exercised by a team of people rather than by one single individual (Acts 20:17; 1 Tim. 5:17; Titus 1:5; James 5:14; 1 Peter 5:1–4).

Cumulatively, the references to the elders indicate that they were in charge of the pastoral care of the congregations. This means that the standard for the early churches was to have a team of pastors rather than only one. Since the lines were not clearly drawn between clergy and laity, some of those leaders were self-supporting while the remuneration of others varied with the degree of their involvement in ministry (1 Tim. 5:17). There is no reason for this model not to remain valid for present-day churches as pastors share leadership with teams of lay leaders trained by them for this very purpose.

In addition to overseers and/or elders, two churches are mentioned as having deacons (Phil. 1:1; 1 Tim. 3:8, 12). Whatever their functions may have been, their services were also provided on the basis of shared leadership since they are always mentioned in the plural. The only exception relates to one "deacon of the church in Cenchrea," who is singled out by name. However, the grammatical form of the text indicates that she was one of several deacons in her community (Rom. 16:1 NRSV).

Throughout the New Testament, church leadership is presented as a collective ministry. Even when the indefinite term "leader" is used in the context of Christian community, it receives a plural reference (Heb. 13:7, 17). Both Timothy and Titus were entrusted with high levels of individual responsibility at Ephesus and in Crete, but neither of them may be counted among the local leadership of those churches. They both had been assigned to those ministries as temporary envoys, to resolve specific problems (1 Tim. 1:3; Titus 1:5). Paul requested both of them to leave their post soon after they had instituted the reforms that they had been sent to implement (cf. 2 Tim. 4:9; Titus 3:12). In both places, their mandate had been to establish teams of reliable leaders. For Christian communities, the best leadership is team leadership.

Team leadership is not a human invention. Its precedent has been set in heaven. The Scriptures present an amazing example of collaborative leadership at the highest level with respect to a church task that seems simple enough: equipping local bodies with spiritual gifts. Because the church since Pentecost is under the general watchcare of the Holy Spirit, it would seem that the distribution of spiritual gifts would simply devolve to the Holy Spirit. However, all three persons of the Godhead are closely involved together in endowing the church with spiritual gifts. The Holy Spirit provides the gifts; Christ the Lord provides different kinds of service; and God the Father supplies different kinds of working (1 Cor. 12:4–6).

The church and its local ministry are important enough in God's purposes for the whole Trinity to be involved in providing all that is necessary to promote their development. This is collective ministry at its best. The least that can be done by the earthly beneficiaries of this heavenly collaboration is to emulate it and to oppose resolutely any autocratic commandeering of leadership within Christian communities.

Headship

No human is ever designated in Scripture as sole leader of a church or as its head. No allowance is ever made in Scripture for any individual to proclaim himself as head of the church. That headship belongs to Christ alone. But even Christ does not appeal to his headship to claim authority over his church. The Scriptures consistently present his headship with regard to the church as a servant function, whereby he provides the church with fullness (Eph. 1:22–23), with growth (4:15–16), with salvation (5:23), with a beginning (Col. 1:18), with fullness in him who is the Creator head of every power (2:9–10; cf. 1:16), and with a growth that finds its source in God (2:19). Since Christ submits himself in servant headship as Savior for the church, in return the church submits itself to Christ in reciprocal servant-hood (Eph. 5:23–24). No church leader may function outside of this servant subjection. Christ treats the church as his bride— never as his slave. Likewise, church leaders must treat the faith-ful as fellow-servants, never as subordinates.

The New Testament use of the concept of "head" crystallizes the biblical definition of leadership. As the preeminent part of the body, the head can promote itself by insisting on its superior status as chief, boss, ruler, or as one who wields authority over the body. Predictably, the opposite is true in the New Testament. The head is always one who, even if preeminent, serves the body as a source of life, growth, and strength. Biblical headship is a servant function, driven by a passion for meeting needs rather than by the desire to exercise authority over others.

Since a fuller discussion of the New Testament meaning of "head" is available in my book *Beyond Sex Roles* (Baker, 1985; pp. 137–38, 157–62, 215–52, 290–95), only one biblical instance will be cited here to illustrate the pressure exerted by secular culture on the biblical notion of headship to render it as hierarchy instead of servanthood. When the apostle Paul discussed the implications of the origination of man and woman (1 Cor. 11:7–9, 11–12), he began with a statement (v. 3) about the headship of Christ to man (A), of man to woman (B), and of God to Christ (C). With total disregard for the biblical ordering of those three clauses, a glib but popular interpretation of this verse turns it topsy-turvy to make it a hierarchy. A top-down God-Christ-man-woman chain of command is obtained by shifting the clauses around and by rendering "head" as authority—ABC becomes CAB!

However, the biblical order for this verse is not one of hierarchy (CAB) but of servanthood (ABC): The head of every man is Christ because at creation, when all things were made through him, he endowed the man with life (A); then, the head of the woman is man because her life was drawn from the man (B); and finally, the head of Christ is God because God provided the life of the Son at the Incarnation (C). With this sequence that culminates with God, Paul wanted to demonstrate a truth he stated in the immediate context: ultimately, "everything comes from God" (v. 12). Now, man and woman are interdependent in terms of origination (vv. 11–12). But all human beings, including the incarnate Christ, owe their existence to the life-giving headship of God.

This understanding of 1 Corinthians 11:3 provides an explanation for the baffling omission of the Holy Spirit from the sequence. The Holy Spirit would have been necessarily included in a hierarchy of authority between divinity and humankind since he is Christ's Paraclete, ministering on his behalf. According to Scripture, the Godhead has absolute rights of sovereignty over all created beings, and humans must be subject to all three persons of the Trinity. But divine rulership is not the point of this particular passage of Scriptures. The Holy Spirit was left out of the sequence because he is not reported in Scripture as having been involved in the making of either man or woman, and, obviously, only Christ is Son of God. The Holy Spirit is never described as son of the Father or as father of the Son. For this reason, the biblical order of the three clauses (ABC) must be respected as a sequence describing successive relations of headship as origination rather than be reshuffled and forced into the mode of a hierarchy.

The biblical concept of leadership is subsumed in this meaning of "headship": someone who does not misuse a position of preeminence to exercise authority over others, but who acts as a servant provider to strengthen and elevate others. The essence of Christian leadership is the courage to give, not the desire to rule. There will never be enough of such authentic leaders. For any congregation, a plurality of leaders thus motivated is a blessing of God to the church.

In a community composed of mutual servants, no one has the right to play rulership. Leaders in particular are not exonerated from the overall command for all Christians to be in mutual submission and, therefore, in reciprocal servanthood (Eph. 5:21). The New Testament definition of leadership, whether in church or family, always calls for a partnership of shared leadership on the basis of spiritual gifts. As such, the ultimate protection for the integrity of leadership as servanthood is plurality of leadership.

Conclusion

With great hope and with an eye to the fulfillment of his mission on earth, Jesus had poured out his heart to the disciples. For months he had drilled into them the basic principles of the kingdom. By word and deed, with beatitudes and parables, through signs and wonders, he had demonstrated to his followers that, with him in their midst, God had come near them and that the kingdom was among them.

However, along with the crowds, who pressed hard after Jesus and were anxious to receive the benefits of his power, the disciples had been perplexed about his real identity. They exclaimed in wonderment at his authority and at the power of his teaching. But they had been unable to discern in him the one who held the power to restore their relationship with God and their communion with each other.

In order to force the issue, Jesus led the disciples to a retreat at a beautiful resort village in northern Galilee. In this quiet setting, away from the demands of ministry and from the pressures of the crowds, Jesus became expansive with the disciples and more directly personal. With keen anticipation, he guided the conversation toward the crucial issue of their understanding of his identity. "Who do you say I am?" he asked expectantly (Matt. 16:15). He knew that their eternal destiny and the success of his mission on earth depended on their accurate perception of him and of his ministry.

At long last and in a flash of divine inspiration, Peter heard himself exclaim, "You are the Christ, the Son of the living God" (v. 16). The obvious truth that had been staring at them from the beginning was finally recognized. Jesus sighed with relief. His earthly mission was now secure.

Jesus's response to this first instance of human recognition of his supernatural identity was an exclamation of blessedness. He envisioned the transformation of ordinary individuals like Simon into the building blocks of the new community. For the first time, he solemnly announced that *he* would build *his* church and that this new community would prevail against the forces of hell because it would hold the keys of access to the kingdom of God. At the very moment of his recognition as the fulfiller of God's designs for humanity, Jesus embraced for all generations the multitude of those who would believe in him, and he bonded them together into a new community he called "my church"—his most precious possession on earth and into eternity (vv. 17–19).

A generation later, reflecting on the relationship of Christ with his church, the great apostle exclaimed: "Christ loved the church and gave himself up for her" (Eph. 5:25). God so loved the world that he gave his only Son, but the Son so loved the church that he gave his life for her.

Jesus Christ was the love expression of the Godhead. He loved life; he had created it. He loved people; they were the object of his ministry. He loved his disciples; he called them his friends. He loved the rich young ruler; he wanted him for a disciple. He loved the Father; together with the Holy Spirit, they were the original community of oneness. He loved John, the beloved disciple. He loved Lazarus, to the point of refusing his death. He loved Mary and Martha as his own sisters. He loved the world of nature; it had come out of his creator hands. Christ had many loves. But the dominant love of his life was his love for the church, his bride. His life was driven by a compelling, irresistible passion for the church. He loved the church to death. His love for her is inalterable. She will remain his bride in all eternity.

Anyone who claims to love Christ without loving the church that Christ loves does not really love Christ. When authentic, love for Christ necessarily translates into love for the church (1 John 4:20–21). The hermit who cultivates spirituality in the remote solitude of a cave does not really love Christ. The evangelist who thinks he saves and heals people without pressing them to join the church does not really love Christ. The priest who claims to be the church does not really love Christ. The parachurch staffer who remains unchurched does not really love Christ. A boring preacher does not really love Christ. A passive church attender does not really love Christ. A competitive church planter does not really love Christ. An irascible missionary does not really love Christ. A racist, sexist Christian does not really love Christ. A greedy Christian does not really love Christ. Leaders who shackle ministry with hierarchy do not really love Christ. Christians who allow churches to wallow in mediocrity do not really love Christ. Able-bodied Christians who watch TV evangelists instead of joining local congregations do not really love Christ.

He or she loves Christ who, like him, is willing to sacrifice blood for the church in order to help present her to him as a radiant church, without stain or wrinkle or any other blemish but holy and blameless. One who really loves Christ is driven by a compelling passion for the church because she is his passion.

Because they are caught in ecclesiastical systems that perpetuate themselves unchallenged, many well-meaning Christian leaders and their followers unthinkingly promote forms of church organization that are blatantly anti-church. Relating a personal experience will help illustrate the point.

While visiting friends in a large metropolitan center in the United States, I was invited to attend a Sunday morning service with them at their church. As we walked toward the entrance of the building, we were greeted by a group of affable people who welcomed us warmly and who asked me, as a newcomer, to register my name on a guest book. Inside the large narthex, we were met by an usher who guided us to a pew, where we sat and waited for the service to begin. While waiting, I observed in the pew immediately in front of us a beautiful family dressed in their Sunday best. The young boy was seated next to his father and his two sisters, on the other side, next to their mother.

As the church filled up, the organ prelude gave way to more stately music and five solemn-looking people came in, marching in step down the center aisle. They made their way up on the platform and sat in large armchairs, facing the congregation. Soon the service began, and they took turns in leading the congregation through its various parts. At one point, one of them announced the offering and asked for the offering-takers to come forward. From all over the sanctuary, a number of people walked to the platform, took the offering baskets, and started moving through the pews.

It was then that it hit me. I suddenly realized that, beginning with the greeters at the door, the people involved in any ministry capacity as greeters, ushers, worship leaders, and now collection-takers had all been men. Not one woman had done anything of visible significance apart from sitting in the pews. It dawned on me that I was actually watching the rituals of gender religion.

After the sermon, which I could follow only distractedly, one of the pastors announced communion and asked for the communion servers to come forward. Again, a bunch of people came up from all over the congregation. They were all men.

As I sat there, seething with frustration while the symbols of Christ's sacrifice for the oneness of the church were being abused, I considered the family sitting in front of me. With outrage mounting within me, I wondered. By what right could this church, in the name of Christ, beat into the consciousness of this woman and of her two daughters the demeaning conviction of their inadequacy as full participants in the work of ministry because of their womanhood? By what right could this church ravage their personhood in Christ and relegate them to the status of second-class citizens of the kingdom because they were born female? By what right was the free use of the spiritual gifts that had been lavished by the Holy Spirit on the people in this congregation denied to the kingdom?

By what right was this church taking the risk of alienating forever from the faith those two little girls who, someday, would reject the church because of the spiritual abuse to which they were now being subjected in the name of Christ? By what right was this church inculcating in this little boy a false sense of his superiority as a male and preparing him to perpetuate the odious, brutalizing dysfunction as a grown-up man?

By what right could this church betray its sacred calling as the community of oneness? By what right could this church inflict upon its own people the preferential treatment that the Scripture explicitly forbids Christians to practice even toward outsiders (James 2:1–6)? By what right could this church send missionaries "to travel over land and sea to win a single convert" and make him twice as much a victim of a caste system not much different from the practice of his own heathen religion?

Of course, in that state of mind, partaking of communion was out of the question. All I could do was to grieve silently and wait for the end of the service. But the end was not yet to come. Following communion, one of the pastors announced that this was a special day for the church since they were commissioning a missionary for service in Africa. He explained that this particular missionary assignment called for church planting and leadership development. He then asked the missionary to come up on the platform. To my great surprise, a woman rose from the front pew and walked to the platform. She was offered a chair and sat down, conspicuously alone and silent. The pastor then asked the elders and ministry leaders to come up on the platform and to join the pastoral staff for prayer. From all over the congregation, a crowd of people gathered around the woman so that she was no longer visible, and they took turns praying up a storm, asking God to bless her ministry among the "natives." Not one woman was among them, praying for her. They were all white men, asking God to bless her ministry to the blacks in Africa.

Again, I shrunk down into the pew, confounded by the blatant inconsistency of the situation. A woman was not good enough to do any visible form of ministry in this white, male-dominated congregation, but it was okay for her to be a church planter and a leader far away from them, among black Christians. In their blindness to their own inconsistency, these churchgoers did not realize that their sinful discrimination against the women among them was surpassed only by their sin of racial prejudice.

However, with a renewed sense of my own sinfulness, I realized that all those well-meaning Christians were giving in to the pretense because they were themselves victims of a system. They were like puppets acting out a travesty of community, thinking that their pathetic parody was the real thing. They did not know the biblical alternative to their charade. They had been reading their Bibles without ever being seized by the passion of Christ for the church, without perceiving the grandeur and the beauty of God's design for community, and without understanding the joy and the goodness of relationships of acceptance, of mutuality, and of reciprocal servanthood. All they knew was hierarchy and rulership. For them, church organization was the extension of corporate structures borrowed from the pagan world. Regimentation masquerading as community.

The careful reader of the preceding chapters will have gleaned numerous applications for the recovery and the development of community. A few additional recommendations are listed below for seekers after biblical community.

- Discover or recover from Scriptures the definition of authentic community. Read eagerly through the New Testament in search of holistic definitions of community and of broad principles applicable to its functioning. Pursue such a study until you recognize that community is not a human invention or a survival device, but that it is a gift of God to humans, an essential component of his image grounded in his triune being. Then, develop a passion for community and nurture commutual relationships within family and among friends, small groups, and church and ministry teams. Community is not an optional luxury; it is a binding mandate from God.
- Watch out for religious manifestations of the humanistic scourge of individualism. Note the preponderance of hymns, gospel songs, and praise choruses in the "I, me, and mine" pronoun forms instead of those that celebrate com-

munity with "we, us, and our." Beware of allowances made for individual worshipers to do their own thing during corporate worship, as if they were having their private devotions but together, in the same location. When worshipers come together to isolate themselves into their own private ecstatic or mystical world and act as if no one else were around, they engage in something that is not true corporate worship as defined in Scripture.

According to the New Testament, a key element of corporate worship is meaningful participation that results in mutual edification. This is essentially the apostle Paul's burden in his discussion of worship in 1 Corinthians 14. As one prays to God in a community setting, even his or her prayer must be meaningful and edifying to those standing by (1 Cor. 14:16–17). As believers gather for worship, each one's contribution "must be done for the strengthening of the church" (v. 26). When they worship together "with psalms, hymns and spiritual songs," believers must be aware that they also "speak to one another" (Eph. 5:19). Worshipers who "sing psalms, hymns and spiritual songs with gratitude in [their] hearts to God" do so within a context where the word of Christ dwells in them richly as they "teach and admonish one another with all wisdom" (Col. 3:16).

Corporate worship is not just quantitatively different from private devotions in that a number people get together to commune privately with God. It is qualitatively different. When Christians worship alone, their concern is essentially for an individual blessing. However, when they worship together, the quest for the personal blessing is intentionally extended to include fellow worshipers. Negatively, this means that physical, emotional, and verbal expressions must be critically appraised and severely checked lest they be offensive or disturbing to other worshipers. On the positive side, only that which is pleasing to God and also mutually edifying belongs in the experience of a worshiping community.

- Note also the evangelical emphasis on having a "personal relationship with Christ" and the lack of equivalent popular terminology about cultivating a corporate relationship with Christ as his body. Correspondingly, be aware that piety is too often reduced to a daily "quiet time" and to "journaling" activities that are conducted in isolation. Remember that spiritual growth happens mostly in the context of interactive relations of mutual watchcare and of reciprocal accountability.

  Obviously, the pursuit of personal spiritual disciplines is highly desirable, but not when it is reduced to self-absorbed, introspective, legalistic exercises. The ultimate purpose for individual piety is to enrich the life of the community and to bring biblical "fullness" to it rather than to become a substitute for it. According to Scripture, Christ "gave himself for us to redeem us" as individuals. But that is only part of the story. Ultimately, he gave himself for the purpose of creating "a people that are his very own," a people with a passion for ministry, "eager to do what is good" (Titus 2:14). Authentic redemption moves from personal salvation to inclusive fullness in community and in corporate ministry (1 Peter 2:2, 4–5, 9).

- Resist current pressures to replace community values with "family values." Apart from a more inclusive community, the family unit cannot withstand on its own the assaults of anti-community forces loose in society. To focus on the family is fine. However, trying to strengthen the family without equal emphasis on the church as its supportive community is misleading and self-defeating.

  The New Testament absolutizes the church as God's ultimate community, but it never absolutizes marriage or family. Indeed, the church has an eternal destiny, but the family is a temporal arrangement that will not be perpetuated in heaven (Matt. 22:30). All believers become automatically members of the body of Christ (1 Cor. 12:12–13), but not all believers are called to be married and to form families

(Matt. 19:12; 1 Cor. 7:7–8, 27, 32–35). Christ made it shockingly clear that discipleship takes precedence over family loyalties (Luke 14:25–27) and that the community of those who do his will is his real family (Mark 3:31–35).

Because God is oneness, the Holy Spirit within us loves oneness. Christian oneness happens when the Spirit within a believer connects with the Spirit in another believer. When hindrances to the gravitational pull of the Spirit get in the way of that part of ourselves that seeks community, the Spirit is grieved and oneness does not happen. But the oneness connection occurs naturally whenever the Spirit within us is allowed to get past the garbage of fear, competition, hierarchy, and jealousy that keeps us apart or makes us enemies. Then, the Spirit is set free to create the oneness that fulfills the need described on the first page of this book.

Thus, through the synergy of the Spirit responding to Spirit, a husband and wife can experience the miracle of oneness. But the Spirit-created circle of oneness cannot be contained within this narrow confinement of the nuclear family. By its very nature, fractional oneness yearns for the inclusiveness, for the affirmation, and for the supportive strength of the larger family of God, the church—apart from which the nuclear family does not have biblical integrity.

Whenever church congregations live out their calling as biblically functioning communities, they inspire, strengthen, and protect the families within their fellowship. Apart from inclusion within the community life of the family of God, Christian families can only muddle their way through lonely desolation. By modeling servant relationships across the board and in all areas of their ministries, church communities will help families live by this one relational practice that can provide a stable foundation to their home life.

However, churches that render lip service to family values while maintaining structures of dominance and exclusion sow the seeds of confusion and dysfunction. Often, they must resort to the expedient of pushing separate men's programs and women's support groups in order to resolve problems thus created—only to find that such disjunctions aggravate the confusion and the alienation.

For instance, huge efforts are being expanded today to encourage Christian men to act as responsible and loyal husbands. But because those programs involve men together in structures of mutual accountability without including their wives as the individuals primarily concerned, they show little understanding of biblical truth about community and have limited impact beyond providing opportunities for great times of male bonding. The biblical model for community life derived from Acts and the New Testament letters is for churches to function as authentic communities by providing natural settings for supportive and cohesive small groups that include and unite couples instead of separating them. Separate men's ministries and women's programs have validity only when they supplement integrated small group programs instead of replacing them. Otherwise, they become a self-defeating substitute to inclusive community life within the local church.

According to the New Testament, the church is "God's household," the basic family of God that embraces smaller family units within it as well as people bereft of family relationships in the all-encompassing oneness of servant love (Eph. 2:19). Therefore, community has priority. Try to shore up the family by itself and it will continue to flounder. But focus on community and the family will flourish.

- To be truly biblical, a belief system should emphasize what the New Testament emphasizes and minimize what the New Testament minimizes. There is no statement in the New Testament that enjoins or permits any Christian to exercise authority over another Christian. In fact, such a practice is categorically forbidden (Matt. 20:25–26; 23:8–12; Mark 10:42–43; Luke 22:25–26). However, there is much teaching in the New Testament that commands all

Christians to be submitted to one another in mutual servanthood. Consequently, in the Christian communities of church and family, relationships of reciprocal submission and servanthood must prevail and receive considerably more emphasis than any structures of authority.

In actual practice, this means that each Christian is duty-bound by biblical imperative to treat other believers as if they were "better" than himself or herself—not just equal but superior (Phil. 2:3). Apart from persons under church discipline, this rule prevails without exceptions for relationships among adult believers in church and family. This is a sure-fire formula for fulfilling the biblical command to accept one another as Christ has accepted us (Rom. 15:7).

Although Christ as Lord is infinitely superior to us, he became servant for our sakes (Phil. 2:6–7). When "Jesus knew that the Father had put all things under his power, and that he had come from God and was returning to God" he nonetheless stooped at the feet of his disciples and acted as their servant—as if *they* were his superiors (John 13:3–5). His command was for his followers to treat each other in the same manner (vv. 13–17). Not rulership but servanthood. Not headship as wielding authority, but headship as serving in humility.

- Expect and demand to utilize your spiritual gifts without hindrance within the context of community. Each Christian is directly accountable to God for his or her acceptance of salvation. Likewise, each Christian is directly accountable to God for his or her use of spiritual gifts in the work of the kingdom.

The kingdom is like a master who entrusted talents to his servants and later called them to settle accounts. The servants who had used their talents were profusely commended and rewarded. However, the one who had failed to use his talent was mercilessly reprimanded as a "worthless servant" and was cast from the master's presence "into the outer darkness, where there will be weeping and gnashing of teeth" (Matt. 25:14–30).

The sobering truth of this parable is that God will hold each believer individually accountable for failure to invest fully his or her giftedness into ministry. God will not question some pastor or priest about our failure. It is our personal responsibility to find the environment or place of service where our talents can be invested without hindrance, to the full extent of our gifting. According to Jesus' parable, excuses will not be tolerated because the work of the kingdom deserves nothing less than the total commitment of all its members.

Conversely, abusive institutions should realize that whenever they choose to stifle God's gifts instead of celebrating them, they incur the frightful responsibility of opposing the Holy Spirit, the provider of such gifts (1 Cor. 12:7, 11). The God-honoring institutional response to God's bountiful provision to the church is acceptance and affirmation of all spiritual gifts—not their rejection and repression.

• Therefore, no church may assume the right to deny a believer the use of his or her spiritual gift once it has been recognized and affirmed in the body. In the context of the most extensive discussion of spiritual gifts in the New Testament, it is made clear that no member of the body may discharge oneself from the responsibility of participating in its functioning (1 Cor. 12:14–20). Likewise, no one may prevent someone else from exercising his or her stewardship of a ministry (vv. 21–25), since all ministries are apportioned by the Holy Spirit (vv. 7, 11). Even the head of the body has no authority to hinder or reject the contribution of its lowliest member (v. 21). The New Testament ideal for the proper functioning of the church as community is maximal participation in the ministry of the totality of the constituency. No excuses and no exclusions.

Of course, in cases of congregational dysfunction, such as those reflected in the Pastoral Letters, there must be retrenchment for local leadership to gain control of critically self-destructive church situations. But the purpose for such institutional control is not to perpetuate itself as a permanent status quo. As illustrated by the diagram below, the spiritual dynamic of change flows from institutional control as a temporary remedial provision toward the biblical ideal of total communal participation.

Because of variable factors pertaining to the history and life of each congregation, specific churches may find themselves at different points on the continuum, from remedial to normative. In fact, the remedial model may be better suited for new church plants as they attempt to establish their corporate identity under the guidance of directive leadership. But there can be no justification for any congregation to remain stuck in the remedial mode. The purpose for the remedial measures such as those prescribed in the Pastoral Letters is to move congregations away from that phase and toward the ideal of total participation in ministry of all the constituency.

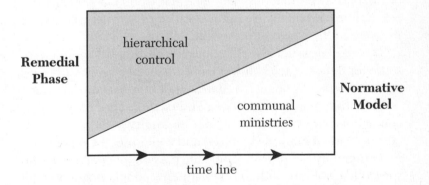

This method for the rehabilitation of sick congregations was precisely what the apostle Paul wanted Titus to "teach" and "stress" in the churches of Crete (Titus 2:14–15; 3:8). Such efforts would be used by Christ to "purify for himself a people that are his very own" (2:14). As a result, the renewed congregations would begin to recover a passion for ministry since they would become "eager to do what is good" (2:14) and would be "careful to devote themselves to doing what is good" (3:8). As unpalatable as they may seem, the purpose for the restrictive measures is to bring dysfunctional congregations back to good health and to enable them to perform their rightful ministry.

The fact that Paul was urging women in the churches of Crete to become teachers (2:3) while all the women in Ephesus were still forbidden to teach (1 Tim. 2:12) indicates that the Cretan congregations were moving faster than the Ephesian church away from hierarchy and closer to the normative model of communal participation. The same movement toward total participation in ministry should characterize all healthy churches.

Most Christians who read their Bibles understand community and desire to experience it. However, for many who are affiliated with strongly hierarchical and authoritarian churches, community remains an elusive, unattainable ideal. Not aware of the fact that a biblical alternative is available and practicable, they often resign themselves to accept the unacceptable and make the best of their abusive situations. The fact that God's blessing can still reach them through anti-community church structures gives a measure of the power of his grace.

The good news for such Christians is that they do not have to settle for defeat. Each believer can be a change agent within his or her sphere of influence, regardless of how insignificant one's contribution may appear to be. The passion for community is contagious. Our innate need for community is so intense that once a spark of interest is ignited and a glimpse of God's dream for community is captured, a burning passion for community can spread like wildfire. When this happens, people begin, in true revival form, to tend their private communion with God. Then they clean up their church and family relationships. They seek to become servants to others, to be sensitive to needs, to meet other people's desires and wants, to care and to share, to give and to receive, to forgive and to be forgiven. They begin to establish relations of mutual support and see them grow into small groups and into ministry teams energized by a common vision.

Gradually, without stress or trauma, the most resistive and entrenched congregation can be changed under the quiet impact of the Holy Spirit. One planted seed of authentic community initiative can result in unpredictable growth that will cause a dead congregation to be transformed into a thriving, outreaching, radiating center of Christian love. *Ecclesia reformata semper reformanda*. The church that has been reformed needs always to be reformed. Authentic revival is always a revival of community life.

An abundance of excellent resources is now available that can provide guidance to thoughtful Christians in their study of the nature and the workings of authentic, biblically functioning communities. Experienced consultants are also available to advise traditional, authority-bound churches about making the transition to communal and participatory forms of congregational life. Other consultants can share their expertise about planting new churches that follow a community pattern from their inception. Several churches that have successfully established a model of community are willing to share their experience through the medium of conferences. These are excellent opportunities for churchgoers in quest of community to attend, listen, observe, ask questions, and learn. The inspiration received at such conferences is often life-changing for the attendees and determinant for their churches. A number of those conferences are open not only to members of the clergy but also to laypeople.

Among several such programs, the Willow Creek Association offers a Christian Leadership Conference several times a year on the campus of the Willow Creek Community Church in the Chicago area. Attendees are not only exposed to the life of a thriving community that endeavors to conform to biblical norms, but they also have access to instructional and inspirational presentations and to workshops about the building of biblically functioning communities. Thousands of pastors, church leaders, and laypeople have witnessed to the fact that their attendance at those conferences was used by God to transform their congregations into God-honoring communities.

It is in connection with a happening at Willow Creek Community Church that this discussion will come to an end. Once
more, the reader's indulgence is requested for a personal narra-
tion. It is hoped that, by contrast with the story about the church
service recounted above, another real-life account will illustrate
the values and the workings of a biblically functioning community. The story is presented here not with the intent of boasting
about human endeavors or glorifying one particular church, but
as an illustration of what can happen when a congregation is
freed up and fired up to use their spiritual gifts for the kingdom.

At the end of a service, I was standing at the back of the audi-
torium, watching thousands of worshipers linger and joyfully fellowship together while making their way out of the building.
Suddenly, I felt someone tapping me on the shoulder. I turned
and saw a shy, plain-looking woman with two small children
standing quietly beside her. She said, "Dr. B, I want to thank the
people of this church. It saved our lives." Thinking that she was
referring to spiritual commitments, I asked, "So, is this where
you became a Christian?" She answered, "Yes, that and much
more. This church saved us from starvation and sure death."
Intrigued by her statement, I asked her what she meant. In a flat,
monotone voice, without show of emotion, she told the following story:

> Somebody my husband met in a bar invited us to go to church
> with him and his wife. He said this church was different and that
> we would like it. We did. The children loved their programs. We
> began attending every week, and I received Jesus as my Savior.
> But a year and a half ago, my husband left me without warning
> and ran away with a woman he knew from work. He took the car
> and left us with two months' rent due on the apartment. The tele-
> phone had already been cut off. There was no money and almost
> no food. I was alone with two small kids.
>
> I went through a very hard time. I couldn't call anyone or go
> anywhere. I had never been on welfare before. I didn't even
> know who to talk to. Our neighbors went to work every day. The
> three of us sat alone in that empty building, crying all the time.
> Soon, we became hungry. The children were asking for food. I

became sad and could do nothing. All that came in the mail was bills and letters from lawyers asking for money. It dawned on me that we might die. I was only hoping that the three of us would die at the same time.

One evening, I had an idea. I waited for the building to become quiet and, in the middle of the night, I went out to the garbage bins. I learned to move my neighbors' garbage from one bin to another and gather leftovers that we could eat. But I felt depressed and wanted to die.

Then, a miracle happened. One evening, the buzzer rang. When I opened the door, an angel of the Lord was standing there. She came in, saw my predicament, and left. That same evening, some people came in and brought a beautiful hot meal. A man and his son brought bags of groceries and children's clothes. They said it was all from the church's food pantry. Two people came with a little stack of twenty dollar bills and said the money was ours. I couldn't believe my eyes, for they were complete strangers to me.

The next day, the rent was paid and the phone reconnected. Two ladies came in, put a set of keys on the table, and said there was a car parked outside that was provided by the car ministry of the church and that it was mine. In the following days, they arranged for child care and gave me leads so I could look for a job. I did find a job, and now we're standing on our own feet. I know we're going to make it. You see, Dr. B, this church saved our lives.

As she was telling her story, I could easily reconstitute what had happened as far as the church was concerned. Under the broad ministry umbrella of the church, more than a hundred subministries are in place, functioning around the clock or ready to respond to emergencies at a moment's notice. Most of those ministries were started because someone in the congregation saw a need, gathered a team of believers with similar gifting and passion around herself or himself, and, under staff coordination, launched a new dimension of outreach or community care sustained by volunteer lay workers.

But I became curious about the identity of the "angel" who had discovered the woman's dismal situation and had triggered the process of interventions. I conducted a discreet inquiry to find out what had caused this person to go to the apartment. I learned that our angel was none other than the Sunday School teacher of one of the children. She had noticed the child's absence and had tried to reach the family over the phone. Upon learning that the phone had been disconnected, she assumed that they had moved away and removed the card from the file. But she had established the habit of praying through the roster of children periodically. Each time she came to the name of this child, she felt a strange unrest within her. Although the toddler and his family were out of her life, she could not bring the matter to closure. She tried to call again but without results. Finally, she got up one morning, pulled out the family's address, located it on a map, and in the evening, after work, drove over—just in case.

The chain reaction of rapid interventions that was triggered by the Sunday School teacher's visit would hardly have occurred in a rigidly hierarchical church hampered by exclusive ministry structures and subject to clerical dominance. In the hierarchical church described above, the greater part of the congregation had been marginalized into insignificance. As a result, its sub-ministries were few in number and pathetically limited in scope. Freedom to fulfill ministry according to one's spiritual gifts was considered a male privilege divinely granted only to one gender. Under such limitations, ministry becomes predictably stunted, compassion shrivels, and outreach turns into a burdensome constraint rather than the exuberant response of love spontaneously and cooperatively expressed in the full measure of each one's gift.

However, let ministry be recognized not as the privileged purview of the few but as the divine call for all to invest themselves fully and joyfully in the work of the kingdom, and watch community flourish and expand irrepressibly. Watch community take on the powers of hell; subdue the rulers, the authorities, the powers of this dark world, and the spiritual forces of evil in the heavenly realms; and bring them bound and screaming for mercy under the transcendental, heaven-and-earth sovereignty of our Lord Jesus Christ.

Appendix

Hermeneutical Bungee-Jumping: Subordination in the Godhead

GILBERT BILEZIKIAN*

Students of the history of Christian thought generally believe that hermeneutical deviations from what evangelicals consider to be orthodox doctrine do not appear as the result of premeditated conspiracies to create new heresies. Such aberrations creep into the belief systems of the Church imperceptibly carried by degrees into the corporate religious consciousness through concerns that often appear legitimate. The purpose of this presentation is to bring to the attention of evangelical scholars a hermeneutical approach to the doctrine of the Trinity that is being developed in our midst and that, I believe, stretches our tolerance for theological innovation beyond the limits of orthodoxy.

Ever since the formulation of the Nicene and Chalcedonian affirmations the Church, at least in its post-Augustinian expression, has rested securely in its understanding of the Trinity as it was interpreted by the councils and defined in the creeds. Occasionally some aspect of the doctrine of the Trinity comes under attack at the hands of sectarians. But Biblical Christians have been quick to rise to its defense and to guard it against redefinitions and new interpretations.

The Evangelical Theological Society (ETS) provides a striking contemporary example of this conservative reflex. Since its inception, the ETS had been content to maintain the following sentence as its doctrinal basis: "The Bible alone, and the Bible in its entirety, is the Word of God written and is therefore inerrant in the autographs." For decades this one-sentence creed served the Society satisfactorily. In recent years, however, it became necessary to expand it in order to protect the Society

*Gilbert Bilezikian is professor emeritus at Wheaton College, 501 East College Avenue, Wheaton, IL 60187. This article is reprinted, with permission, from the *Journal of the Evangelical Theological Society* 40/1 (March, 1997): 57–68.

from infiltration by deviant views of the Trinity. To the existing sentence was added another: "God is a Trinity, Father, Son and Holy Spirit, each an uncreated person, one in essence, equal in power and glory." With this addendum the ETS resoundingly affirmed the historic view of the Trinity. It recognized the oneness of the Godhead along with the eternity, the ontological identity and the equality in authority or sovereignty ("power") and honor or status ("glory") among the three persons of the Trinity.

At this point, one wishes it were possible to be assured that all is well with the doctrine of the Trinity and that this theological legacy is scrupulously protected inside the evangelical camp. Unfortunately this is not so. From within our own ranks a potentially destructive redefinition of the doctrine of the Trinity is being developed that threatens its integrity at what has historically proven to be its most vulnerable point: the definition of the relationship between the Father and the Son. The promoters of this approach are not heretics bent on subverting the faithful. They are well-meaning but overzealous guides who venture into the dangerous waters of Christological speculation only obliquely, while attempting to press other issues. It is possible that, in their eagerness to prove their point, they do not even realize that they may be found tampering with the Church's historic commitment to trinitarian doctrine.

More pointedly, our reference is to the current discussion regarding gender roles in church and family. Some proponents of a hierarchical order between male and female attempt to use, as a divine model for their proposal at the human level, an alleged relationship of authority/subordination between Father and Son. Then a parallel is drawn between a hierarchical order that makes the Son subordinate to the Father to a hierarchical order that makes women subordinate to men, thus claiming theological legitimacy for the latter. It is not within the parameters of this presentation to enter into the gender roles debate. Our discussion will focus essentially on the theory of the subordination of the Son to the Father.

After the Arian controversy and its settlement at the councils, the western Church affirmed the consubstantiality of the Son and the Holy Spirit with the Father, the coeternality and the essential oneness of the persons of the Trinity, thus excluding any form of ontological hierarchy, order or ranking among them that would pertain to their eternal state. But while the Church affirmed the full divinity of Christ in both his nature and status, it also recognized that a radical disruption took place within the Trinity in relation to human history. After declaring in lofty terms that the Lord Jesus Christ is "true God from true God, begotten, not made, of one substance with the Father through whom all things came into existence," the creed goes on to state that he, "because of us men, and because of our salvation, came down from heaven and was incarnate from the Holy Spirit and the Virgin Mary and became man and was crucified for us under Pontius Pilate and suffered, and was buried."

What the creed describes in those majestic cadences is not business as usual for the Trinity but the awesome and tragic travail of divinity from infinity to human brokenness for the purpose of its redemption, as if heaven had been thrown into a state of cosmic emergency, similar to that of a shepherd abandoning his ninety-nine sheep in the desert to go searching for a missing one. In many ways the Scriptures explain that this divine mission of mercy was accomplished at infinite cost for God and that it required an unprecedented and unrepeatable dislocation within the Trinity. In order to minister to humans out of love, and in characteristic servanthood, God in Christ became man.

Within the context of Christ's ministry to the world, and in this context alone, Scripture indeed teaches the complete humiliation of the Son. From the position of equality with the Father, at the pinnacle of divine glory, the Son descended to the most degrading experience of debasement known among humans by suffering the humiliation of a public execution as a criminal. While in this state of humiliation the Son's divine nature was not affected. Although human personhood was added to the divine subsistence of the Son, he remained one in substance with the Godhead. As Christ in his humanity anticipated the joy of returning to the Father, he could state: "The Father is greater than I" (John 14:28). And as he described his mission to the world he said, "I do as the Father has commanded me" (14:31). When Christ the servant described his mission as not seeking to do his own will but the will of the Father who had sent him, he confessed: "I can do nothing on my own authority" (5:30).

But, conversely, Christ on earth could claim complete mutuality with the Father and full equality with him. When asked to reveal the Father, Christ broadly stated: "He who has seen me has seen the Father" (14:9). When he described himself as the source of eternal life and the Father as his warrant, Christ claimed: "I and the Father are one" (10:30). To summarize the claims that Christ made about himself, the gospel writer explained that Christ had made himself equal with God

(5:18). And just prior to his ascension, when the Son was anticipating returning to his heavenly glory, he declared: "All authority in heaven and on earth has been given to me" (Matt 28:18).

So during his earthly life Christ remained a full participant in the Godhead, thereby retaining his divine subsistence. Paradoxically he also made himself subject to the Father when he assumed human personhood. Of course the relation of Christ's divine nature to the human nature assumed by him is a theological issue all its own. It is a separate issue and not of our concern at the moment. Our focus in this discussion is the Scriptures' definition of Christ's subjection when he functioned as Redeemer. The Scriptures qualify his subjection in the following manner.

Christ did not take upon himself the task of world redemption because he was number two in the Trinity and his boss told him to do so or because he was demoted to a subordinate rank so that he could accomplish a job that no one else wanted to touch. He volunteered his life out of sacrificial love. Being born in the likeness of man, he also took the form of a servant and as such became obedient unto death, even death on a cross. Scripture describes this process in these words: "He humbled himself " (Phil 2:8). He was not forced to become a servant; he was not compelled to be obedient; he was not dragged to his death against his will. The Bible puts it tersely: "He humbled himself." Therefore it is much more appropriate, and theologically accurate, to speak of Christ's self-humiliation rather than of his subordination. Nobody subordinated him, and he was originally subordinated to no one. He humbled himself.

A second qualification pertains to Christ's humiliation. The Bible also teaches that the humiliation of the Son was an interim or temporary state. It was not, nor shall it be, an eternal condition. Christ's humiliation was essentially a phase of ministry coincidental with the need of his creatures. From all eternity, and in the beginning, Christ was with God, and Christ was God, and he was in the form of God. He was equal with God, but the time came when he did not consider his equality with God a privilege to clutch as his own. Rather, he let go of it and took the form of a servant. It was something new for him. Being in the form of a servant was not an eternal condition. He took it up. He became obedient unto death. Prior to the incarnation there had been no need for him to be obedient since he was equal with God. But despite the fact that he had the dignity of sonship he learned obedience through what he suffered (Heb 5:8). Obedience was a new experience for him, something he had to learn. It was not an eternal state. When Christ came into the world he said, "Behold, I have come to do your will, O God" (10:5, 7).

The frame of reference for every term that is found in Scripture to describe Christ's humiliation pertains to his ministry and not to his eternal state. When this redemptive ministry draws close to its eschatological consummation, Christ will deliver the kingdom to the Father because God has already put all things under his feet, and one more time the Son will be made subject to the Father so as to bring the work of redemption to a triumphant finale as God becomes all in all (1 Cor 15:24-28). The stated purpose for this last act of subjection of the Son is that God may become all in all and thus bring to completion the redemptive process that had required Christ's humiliation (15:28; Eph 1:23; 4:10). Any inference relative to an eternal state of subjection that would extend beyond this climactic fulfillment is not warranted by this text or any other Biblical text. The nonexistence of such Biblical data is made obvious in an article by John V. Dahms.[1] In an effort to show that the NT teaches the "essential and eternal" subordination of the Son, Dahms forces questionable subordinationist inferences out of texts such as John 17:24; Eph 3:21; Phil 2:9-11; Mark 13:32; 14:62; John 1:1.

At the very end, when Christ's self-subjection will have achieved its redemptive purpose and as he is universally acclaimed as Lord, his reintegration to supreme preeminence will also bring glory to God the Father (Phil 2:11). In other words the Father will highly exalt him, and he will highly glorify the Father. Reciprocity remains the consistent mode of interaction within the Godhead until the end and into eternity.

Because there was no order of subordination within the Trinity prior to the Second Person's incarnation, there will remain no such thing after its completion. If we must talk of subordination it is only a functional or economic subordination that pertains exclusively to Christ's role in relation to human history. Christ's kenosis affected neither his essence nor his status in eternity.

Except for occasional and predictable deviations, this is the historical Biblical trinitarian doctrine that has been defined in the creeds and generally defended by the Church, at least the western Church,

---

[1] J. V. Dahms, "The Subordination of the Son," *JETS* 36/3 (September 1994) 351–364.

throughout the centuries. It is worth reiterating that it has been singularly affirmed in our day by the ETS: "God is a Trinity, Father, Son and Holy Spirit, each an uncreated person, one in essence, equal in power and glory."

Thus it is impossible within the confines of orthodoxy to derive a model for an order of hierarchy among humans from the ontological structure of the Trinity, since all three persons are equal in essence. Moreover, because Christ's functional subjection is not an eternal condition but a task-driven, temporary phase of ministry, it is presented in Scripture as a model of servanthood and mutual submission for all believers (Phil 2:5-11). Because of its temporary character, Christ's subjection does not lend itself as a model for a permanent, generically-defined male/female hierarchy.

Unfortunately some propounders of female subordination cannot let it go at that. In order to make the trinitarian model work for them, they do not hesitate to stretch the concept of Christ's functional subordination from a temporary phase to an eternal condition and to define it not as a temporary necessity required to accomplish the work of redemption but as the eternal status of the Son in relation to the authority of the Father. To be specific, the work of two representatives of this school of thought will be cited and briefly evaluated.

Some of the authors of *Recovering Biblical Manhood and Womanhood* struggle with the definition of "head" as used by the apostle Paul in 1 Corinthians, Ephesians and Colossians.[2] They try to establish that "head" meant "authority over" or "leader" as it does in English, whereas in each of the contexts where it is used "head" in Greek naturally yields the meaning of "servant-provider of life, of growth and fullness" (1 Cor 11:3, cf. 8, 12; Eph 1:22-23; 4:15-16; 5:23; Col 2:19; etc.).

In particular the authors of *Recovering* endow "head" with the meaning of authority in their interpretation of 1 Cor 11:3: "Christ is the head of every man; the husband is the head of the wife, and God is the head of Christ." They insist that this text teaches the existence of an order of hierarchy between God and Christ on one hand and between men and women on the other. Of course they have no satisfactory answer for the fact that Paul's ordering of the three clauses rules out a hierarchical sequence (BCA instead of ABC) and for the fact that the meaning of

---

[2]*Recovering Biblical Manhood and Womanhood* (ed. J. Piper and W. Grudem; Wheaton: Crossway, 1991).

"head" in this statement, as well as in other NT passages where it is similarly used, is better rendered as "one considered preeminent but acting as servant-provider, or source (of life and growth)."[3]

Wayne Grudem states about the clause "the head of Christ is God" (11:3) that it indicates "a distinction in role in which primary authority and leadership among the persons of the Trinity has always been and will always be the possession of God the Father." Again Grudem proffers that God the Son is "eternally equal to the Father in deity and essence, but subordinate to the Father in authority."[4] But even if "head" in this passage were to mean authority, neither the passage nor its context contains any indication that this headship describes an eternal state. In this text Paul is referring to the relationship that prevails between God and Christ in the context of Christ's ministry to men and women within human history.

In the course of this discussion Grudem writes that the doctrine of the "eternal generation of the Son" implies "a *relationship* between the Father and the Son that *eternally* existed and that will always exist-a relationship that includes a subordination in role, but not in essence or being."[5] Grudem has it backwards. By definition the doctrine of eternal generation pertains precisely to "essence or being" since it defines the Son's filiation. It says nothing about roles, much less about subordination.

The doctrine of the eternal generation of the Son, itself a creedal construction subject to aleatory interpretations rather than a strongly attested Biblical motif, and terminology such as Father and Son designations intended to convey ineffable mysteries into the immanency of human language have sometimes given way to simplistic anthropomorphic projections not warranted by Scripture. God is Father, but he never had a wife. Christ is the eternal Son, but he has no mother. Sons are always born within time, but Christ is without a beginning. Fathers are always older than their sons, but Father and Son are eternal. Sons normally outlive their fathers, but the Son and the Father are immortal. In their early years sons are subordinated to their fathers, but Son and Father have been and are eternally "equal in power and glory." Sons are

---

[3]Cf. G. Bilezikian, *Beyond Sex Roles* (Grand Rapids: Baker, 1993) 157–162, 215–252.

[4]*Recovering* 457, 540.

[5]Ibid. 457.

unilaterally dependent on their fathers for their existence, but by definition no member of the Trinity is unilaterally dependent on another for his existence. The oneness structure of the Trinity and its eternalness require that each of its members be constantly dependent upon the other two for the Trinity to exist. The few references to the "only begotten" Son that are invoked to justify a doctrine of eternal generation require a more cautious treatment than to be used to legitimize the concept of an eternal subordination process otherwise not attested in Scripture (John 1:14, 18; 3:16, 18; 1 John 4:9). These would be better understood as referring to the necessity of the incarnation, just as "the Lamb that was slain from the creation of the world" (Rev 13:8) refers to the crucifixion rather than to a theory of Christ's eternal passion. Grudem's notion of the eternal functional subordination of the Son to the Father bears the troubling marks of a reductive anthropomorphism.

In defense of his position Grudem takes to task theologians such as Millard Erickson, who see "subordination in role as non-eternal, but rather a temporary activity of the members of the Trinity for a period of ministry."[6] Grudem's claim that the Son was in eternal functional subordination to the Father, however, also has devastating consequences for *kenōsis* Christology. According to Scripture the Son did surrender a dimension of his equality with the Father in his *kenōsis* (Phil 2:6). Since according to Grudem there was no functional parity to begin with, the only structure of equality left for the Son's "emptying" was his ontological equality with the Father. Inevitably Grudem's theory of the Son's eternal functional subordination leads to an incarnate Christ who was fully divine neither in function nor in essence. Scripture teaches the opposite. In his incarnation the Son remained equal with the Father. But he temporarily forfeited his functional equality to assume the "form of a servant." This was a new mode of being for the Son in relation to the Father, not an eternal state (v. 7).

The other text adduced by Grudem in support of his theory of eternal subordination is Heb 1:3, where it states that when Christ "made purification for sin he sat down at the right hand of the majesty on high." Grudem comments: "Jesus is at the right hand, but God the Father is still on the throne."[7] This is a very revealing statement. There is no mention in Heb 1:3 of any throne in connection with the right

---

[6]Ibid. 540.
[7]Ibid. 457.

hand of God, although there is in 8:1; 12:2. But in the same verse that Grudem uses (1:3) are found some of the strongest ascriptions of the attributes of deity to Christ contained in the NT. It states that the Son is the radiance of God's glory, the exact representation of his being, sustaining all things by his powerful word. Instead Grudem assumes that sitting at the right hand of the throne is a position of subordination. In reality it can be cogently argued from Scripture that it is a position of exaltation to supreme glory. But we concede to Grudem that God's throne is the ultimate transcendental symbol of divine authority.

We discover in Scripture not only that Christ is sitting at the right hand of God but also that he is sitting at the center of God's throne. This is not an incidental reference but a heavy emphasis made especially in the book of Revelation. In Rev 3:21 Christ says, "I overcame and sat down with my Father on his throne." Only Christ may join the Father on his throne. Victorious believers are invited to become guest participants in the reign of Christ on a different throne. In 7:17 the Lamb is at the center of the throne of God. In 12:5 the Son who will rule all the nations with an iron scepter is "taken up to God and to his throne." In 22:3 we are told that there will be one throne in the heavenly Jerusalem, the eternal city of God. It is "the throne of God and of the Lamb." Contrary to Grudem's suggestion, God is not on the throne with the Son apart from him or below the throne in a position of subordination. According to Scripture, both God the Father and God the Son occupy the same throne for eternity. They are "equal in power and glory."

The same willingness to assume the risk of appearing to devalue the sovereignty of Christ for agenda purposes is manifest in an article cited and endorsed by Grudem.[8] In this article Robert Letham tries also to build a case for female subordination through the bias of trinitarian speculation. At first he seems to draw a distinction between the ontological equality within the Trinity and a relation of subordination within the functional or economic Trinity. He states: "In terms of God's actions in the history of redemption and revelation we note a clear order [of hierarchy]."[9]

At this point Letham engages an issue that is simply ignored by Grudem. Letham is probably aware that a subordination that extends into eternity cannot remain only functional but that it also becomes *ipso*

---

[8]Ibid. 540.

[9]R. Letham, "The Man-Woman Debate: Theological Comment," *WTJ* 52/1 (Spring 1990) 68.

facto an ontological reality. Grudem tries to maintain that Christ can remain ontologically equal to the Father while he is subjected to an eternal state of functional subordination to him. Letham seems to see the fallacy in this dichotomy. Since the attribute of eternity inheres in the divine essence, any reality that is eternal is by necessity ontologically grounded. Eternity is a quality of existence. Therefore if Christ's subordination is eternal, as both Grudem and Letham claim, it is also ontological. Letham understands this and faces up to it: "There is not only an order [understand "hierarchy"] in the economy of redemption but also in the eternal ontological relations of the persons of the Trinity." Thus for Letham the functional hierarchy is indicative of the ontological hierarchy that exists eternally within the Trinity. He emphasizes this proposition without inhibition: "The revelation of the economic Trinity truly indicates the ontological Trinity."[10] The eternal ontological status of the Son *vis-à-vis* the Father takes the form of an order that is a relation of authority.

Having ventured this far into the hermeneutical minefields of subordinationism, Letham is too astute a theologian not to be aware of the fact that his view of an ontologically stratified, split-level Trinity leads him straight into the trap of Arianism. In a vain attempt to rescue himself from this danger he gives lip service to the coequality of the members of the Trinity while, astoundingly, denying this equality in the same breath. One can appreciate the dilemma from his statement: "The coequality of the Father, Son and Holy Spirit in the unity of the one God takes the form of an order of subsistence."[11] The confusion is flagrant: "coequality" in the form of an "order of subsistence"—which means an ontologically structured hierarchy. It should be either equality and no hierarchy, or hierarchy and no equality. On one hand, Letham cannot bring himself to sacrifice the oneness of the Godhead. On the other, he is driven to superimpose upon it an order of hierarchy. Incongruously he states again that "the *order of subsistence* in *coequal* unity [is] disclosed to be inherent eternally in God."[12]

Since according to Letham the Son was eternally subordinated to the Father both in essence and in function, one wonders where the equality came from that the Son let go in the *kenōsis*. Eternal subordi-

---

[10]Ibid.

[11]Ibid. 73.

[12]Ibid. (italics mine).

nation precludes equality. The Biblical definition of the *kenōsis* as the Son's refusal to exploit the status of equality he had with the Father attests to the fact that there was no subordination prior to the *kenōsis*.

Because he cannot bring himself to forfeit his classic trinitarian heritage, Letham tries to escape the implications of Arian tritheism intrinsic to his theory of ontologically grounded hierarchy in the Godhead. But he cannot. All his talk about equality in the Godhead does not release him from the dire consequences of his theory of Christ's eternal subordination to the Father. Equality suggests a circle of reciprocity in oneness instead of the tritheistic ladder of hierarchy. But the structure of relationships he and Grudem postulate between the persons of the Trinity is the ladder of hierarchy. Letham gets himself into this predicament by positing that the order of hierarchy between Father and Son "consists in authority and obedience. The Father sends the Son. The Son obeys the Father." Nowhere in Scripture, however, does the Father exercise "authority" over the Son, nor is the Son said to "obey the Father." This is not NT terminology. But in any case Letham goes on to say, "Such is clear in the incarnate life of our Lord." He cites as proof some of the passages of Scripture we have previously touched upon (John 5:19-43; 17:1 ff.; cf. esp. Heb 5:8; 10:5-10).

Such texts, however, teach Christ's self-subjection exclusively in relation to the accomplishment of his redemptive ministry. But Letham engages in lethal speculation. He claims that the relation of authority and obedience that allegedly prevailed during the incarnation reflects the eternal relation of Father and Son. If this were not so, "we would have to say then that we had not received a true revelation of God, that Jesus Christ had not made known to us the true nature of God."[13] Therefore for Letham the state of subordination of the incarnate Christ is characteristic of his relation to the Father throughout eternity. The *kenōsis* is thus stripped of its singularity. It becomes normative, an eternal ontological reality within the Godhead.

Letham offers no support from the Scriptures for this jump of logic, and he cannot because there is no such teaching in the Bible. Indeed the Bible does teach very clearly and abundantly that the incarnation is a revelation and that it has made known to us the true nature of God as love. But never does the Bible teach that the Son is

---

[13]Ibid. 69.

eternally subordinate because he took it upon himself to be the Savior. In fact the Bible teaches precisely the opposite of what Letham proposes. In support of his theory Letham carelessly cites a reference that actually argues against him: "Although he was a Son he learned obedience through what he suffered" (Heb 5:8).

Three remarks must be made about this text. (1) The fact that he learned obedience "although" he was a Son indicates that the nature of his Sonship excluded the necessity of obedience. He learned obedience despite the fact that he was a Son. (2) The fact that he "learned" obedience indicates that it was something new in his experience as Son. Obedience was not a mark of his eternal relation to the Father. He learned it for the purpose of ministry. (3) The fact that he learned obedience "through" what he suffered indicates that obedience was required in relation to his suffering and that it was not an eternal condition. Christ's experience of obedience was confined to his redemptive ministry as suffering servant. Letham's handling of this text suggests that a hermeneutic that serves the promotion of ideology may engender exegetical distortions that turn the Biblical text against itself.

In conclusion, we offer three recommendations.

1. *Do not mess with the Trinity.* Especially, let us not run the risk of being found denigrating the lordship and majesty of Christ instead of exalting him. Let God the Father be our example. After the *kenōsis* he was eager to exalt again his Son to the highest place, to give him the name that is above every name so that at the name of Jesus every knee should bow and every tongue confess that Jesus Christ is Lord, to the glory of God the Father. The supreme exaltation of the Son reflects glory even on the Father. If this is how the Father exalts the Son, may humans do less? By what right do humans assign subordination to the Son when the Father does not? In their efforts to assign a subsidiary role to the Son, subordinationists may actually be found dishonoring the Father. According to Scripture, the Father's desire is that "all may honor the Son just as they honor the Father" (John 5:23). Because Father and Son act cooperatively, they deserve equal honor. To assign a subordinate position to the Son may be an affront to both Son and Father. "He who does not honor the Son does not honor the Father" (5:23).

Through the councils, the Church cut across all speculations to affirm the coeternality, the interdependency and the oneness in substance of the three persons of the Trinity, thus excluding any form of hierarchy, order or ranking among them that would pertain to their eternal state. Once the Church recognized that the participation of each person of the Trinity in the ultimacy of divine oneness is absolute, it became impossible to superimpose an order of hierarchy upon the Godhead without violating the Church's primal belief in the absolute nature of God. The doctrine of an absolute Godhead requires that all its members be absolute. To extend the subordination of the Son into Christ's pre-existence to a time prior to creation and to the incarnation comes dangerously close to Arianism, which also recognizes the deity of Christ but in a subordinated form assumed prior to the creation of the cosmos. Then it becomes impossible to speak of the three persons of the Trinity as being one and equal in essence. Instead we have a tiered formation of three gods ranked by decreasing order of power— not the eternal embrace in oneness of Father, Son and Holy Spirit but the split-level stratifications of a pagan pantheon.

The concept of a split-level Trinity also has devastating consequences for the doctrine of salvation. According to Scripture, the redemptive power of the cross derives from the fact that the One who died on it was fully God. God was in Christ reconciling the world to himself (2 Cor 5:19). The work of redemption required the full involvement of the Godhead, not just a subordinate part of the Trinity. God so loved the world that he gave his one and only Son (John 3:16). He did not give the second-ranking officer of the Trinity, the lower god in an Olympian hierarchy.

It makes a lot of difference whether God in Christ offered his life out of sacrificial love, as the Scriptures affirm he did, or whether Christ acted out of obedience because he had no choice but to subject himself to the authority of the Father. To assume that God gave less than his best and his utmost to redeem his creation trivializes the enterprise of redemption and robs it of its tragic singularity and awesome grandeur. A Christology that minimizes the majesty and lordship of Christ by reducing his ministry to that of a subordinate function or to a ministry accomplished out of subordination must be recognized as a deviation from Biblical truth. A low Christology results in a weak soteriology. Let us not tamper with the doctrine of the Trinity lest we run the risk of devaluing the redemptive ministry of Christ and Christ himself. If some people's belief system requires the subordination of women, they should not build their hierarchy at the expense of Christological orthodoxy.

2. *Let us quit talking about subordination.* It is not Biblical terminology. It smacks of the Arian heresy. Subordination is a word of Latin

derivation (*subordinare*) that governs a transitive verb. You do not merely subordinate; you subordinate someone. Thus the word carries connotations of coercion or obligation by reason of superior force or authority. The notion of such a relationship of subordination in the Godhead is completely foreign to Scripture. Indeed, its content teaches exactly the opposite.

According to Scripture, Father, Son and Holy Spirit are united in a relationship of mutual reverence and deference that expresses itself in reciprocal servanthood. The Father glorifies the Son, the Son glorifies the Father, and the Holy Spirit glorifies both. The Father gives everything he has to the Son, the Son gives everything he is to the Father, and the Spirit serves both in everything. The Father gives all authority in heaven and earth to the Son. The Son delivers the kingdom to the Father and subjects himself to the Father, who puts all things under the Son so that God may be all in all.

The Father is at the forefront of the work of creation, but both the *Logos*/Son and the Spirit are present and involved with the Father in creation. The Son is at the forefront of the work of redemption, but both the Father and the Spirit are present and involved with the Son in redemption. The Spirit is at the forefront of the work of sanctification, but both the Father and the Son are present and involved with the Spirit in the work of sanctification.

Indeed the Son made himself servant both to the Father and to humans in order to accomplish his redemptive work (Matt 20:28; Rom 15:8; Phil 2:7). But this servant function did not make him eternally subordinated either to the Father or to humans. Subordinationists must wrench apart the persons of the Trinity in order to place them on a ladder of hierarchy in relation to each other. Not so for the Bible. It was during the days of his flesh and from his servant ministry that the Son claimed to be equal with God the Father (John 5:18). It was from within his alleged "functional subordination" that Christ claimed that the Father was in him and he in the Father, and that he offered his deeds as proof of their functional oneness (10:38).

Any theory of the Son's subordination to the Father must take into account Christ's claim that his earthly ministry was the outworking of the Father's activity present within him: "It is the Father, living in me, who is doing his work. Believe me when I say that I am in the Father and the Father is in me" (14:10-11). With such statements the incarnate Christ claimed to be in functional oneness with the Father. The Son never acts in functional isolation from the Father. When he casts out demons, he does so by the finger of God and the Spirit of God. Both Father and Spirit are actively involved in the ministry of Christ (Luke 10:20; Matt 12:28). The dead are raised and given life through the conjugated operations of both Father and Son (John 5:21). Jesus' teaching about his relation with the Father obliterated any possible disjunction between his ontological oneness with the Father and an alleged functional autonomy of the Son from the Father. For Christ, it was the Father present within him who was doing his work through the Son. Because the Father, living in Christ and at work in and through Christ, could not be in subordination to himself, any talk about Christ's functional subordination to the Father runs the risk of collapsing into nonsense.

The ministry of world redemption must not be reduced to a little side project that could be delegated to the services of a subordinate deity. According to Scripture, God was in Christ reconciling the world to himself (2 Cor 5:19). The all-encompassing work of world redemption required nothing less than the total involvement of the triune God to achieve it. This joint venture can only be described in terms of functional oneness, not functional subordination. To impose upon it a restrictive concept of functional fragmentation within the Trinity trivializes God's work of salvation and reduces it to "a particular limited purpose," as Letham calls it.[14]

The Church has generally rejected the subordination proposal as a pagan infiltration. After stating that to approach the "economic Trinity as the immanent Trinity, and vice versa" represents a broad consensus within Christian theology, Alister E. McGrath observes that "the most significant restatements of the doctrine of the Trinity within the western tradition date from the twentieth century."[15] The current subordinationist proposal may well fall within the category of such modernistic formulations. Therefore we urge today's Christians to discard the terminology of subordination and to describe the servant ministry of Christ with the beautiful term Scripture assigns to it when it refers to his humiliation. He was not subordinated. He humbled himself—not subordination but self-humiliation.

---

[14]Ibid. 68.
[15]A. E. McGrath, *Christian Theology* (Oxford: Blackwell, 1994) 255, 260.

3. *Let us not use God to push our ideological agendas.* The attempt may vitiate our hermeneutics and cause a theological crash.

I recently heard from his siblings that one of my sons had gone bungee-jumping. When I asked him why he had climbed to a high place, tied a line around his waist, and jumped off into a chasm, he answered: "Just to prove something."

Let us be careful not to use God to prove something. Let the Father be God, let Christ be God, let the Holy Spirit be God—all three in one, "equal in power and glory" for all eternity.

ADDENDUM TO PAGES 193–194

Theories of the "eternal generation" of Christ have often been elaborated with disregard for the fact that Scripture itself provides its own interpretation of statements about the Son's filiation. In the Johanine writings, the immediate context of each reference to the "only begotten" indicates that it was made in relation to Christ's incarnation and to his earthly ministry of revelation and redemption, never to an eternal generation or a process of origination (John 1:14, 18; 3:16, 18; 1 John 4:9).

Moreover, the Gospel of John uses consistently the synonymous expressions about Christ as "coming forth out of God" or "from God," in reference to his incarnation and to his ministry, never in relation to a theory of eternal generation (John 8:42; 13:3; 16:27–28; 17:8). The Christological prediction in Psalm 2:7 (RSV), "You are my son; today I have begotten you," and the prophetic promise in 2 Samuel 7:14, "I will be his father, and he will be my son," are pointedly interpreted in the New Testament as referring to Christ's resurrection ministry and to his resulting messianic enthronement (Acts 13:33–34; Heb 1:3–5). Both the Old and New Testament use Christ's designation of "firstborn" as a title indicating dignity and preeminence rather than origination or birth order (Ps 89:7; Heb 1:6), as attested by the fact that David, its first typological recipient, was not a biological "firstborn" (1 Sam. 16:11; Ps 89:20).

Despite patristic assumptions that have heavily influenced hermeneutical tradition, the New Testament never interprets the statements about Christ's filiation as a doctrine of his eternal generation but always as references to his incarnation, his ministry, and his ensuing exaltation.

Scripture Index

262.7 LINCOLN CHRISTIAN COLLEGE AND SEMINARY   118678

B5957

c.2

RESOURCES

This resource was created to serve you.

It is just one of many ministry tools that are part of the Willow Creek Resources® line, published by the Willow Creek Association together with Zondervan Publishing House. The Willow Creek Association was created in 1992 to serve a rapidly growing number of churches from all across the denominational spectrum that are committed to helping unchurched people become fully devoted followers of Christ. There are now more than 2,500 WCA member churches worldwide.

The Willow Creek Association links like-minded leaders with each other and with strategic vision, information, and resources in order to build prevailing churches. Here are some of the ways it does that:

- **Church Leadership Conferences**—3 1/2 -day events, held at Willow Creek Community Church in South Barrington, IL, that are being used by God to help church leaders find new and innovative ways to build prevailing churches that reach unchurched people.

- **The Leadership Summit**—a once-a-year event designed to increase the leadership effectiveness of pastors, ministry staff, volunteer church leaders, and Christians in business.

- **Willow Creek Resources®**—to provide churches with a trusted channel of ministry resources in areas of leadership, evangelism, spiritual gifts, small groups, drama, contemporary music, and more. For more information, call Willow Creek Resources® at 800/876-7335. Outside the US call 610/532-1249.

- *WCA News*—a bimonthly newsletter to inform you of the latest trends, resources, and information on WCA events from around the world.

- *The Exchange*—our classified ads publication to assist churches in recruiting key staff for ministry positions.

- **The Church Associates Directory**—to keep you in touch with other WCA member churches around the world.

- *WillowNet*—an Internet service that provides access to hundreds of Willow Creek messages, drama scripts, songs, videos and multimedia suggestions. The system allows users to sort through these elements and download them for a fee.

- *Defining Moments*—a monthly audio journal for church leaders, in which Lee Strobel asks Bill Hybels and other Christian leaders probing questions to help you discover biblical principles and transferable strategies to help maximize your church's potential.

For conference and membership information please write or call:

Willow Creek Association   ph: (847) 765-0070
P.O. Box 3188   fax: (847) 765-5046
Barrington, IL 60011-3188   www.willowcreek.org

3 4711 00181 5333